CONFESSIONS

www.**transworldbooks**.co.uk

CONFESSIONS

SIMON MAYO

Deep, dark secrets from a new
generation of sinners as heard on
BBC Radio 2's DRIVETIME

BANTAM PRESS

LONDON • TORONTO • SYDNEY • AUCKLAND • JOHANNESBURG

TRANSWORLD PUBLISHERS
61–63 Uxbridge Road, London W5 5SA
A Random House Group Company
www.transworldbooks.co.uk

First published in Great Britain
in 2011 by Bantam Press
an imprint of Transworld Publishers

A CIP catalogue record for this book
is available from the British Library.

ISBN 9780593069370

Addresses for Random House Group Ltd companies outside the UK
can be found at: www.randomhouse.co.uk
The Random House Group Ltd Reg. No. 954009

The Random House Group Limited supports The Forest Stewardship
Council (FSC®), the leading international forest-certification organization.
Our books carrying the FSC label are printed on FSC® certified paper.
FSC is the only forest-certification scheme endorsed by the leading
environmental organizations, including Greenpeace. Our paper
procurement policy can be found at
www.randomhouse.co.uk/environment

Typeset in Giovanni, Versailles and Fairfield
by Falcon Oast Graphic Art Ltd.
Printed and bound in Great Britain by
CPI Group (UK) Ltd, Croydon, CR0 4YY

2 4 6 8 10 9 7 5 3 1

For my children, Ben, Natasha and Joe,
who assure me they have nothing to confess.

Contents

Introduction

Well, here we are again – let the strains of Albinoni's Adagio ring out once more. Confessions started on Radio 1 in August 1990 with the intention that it would run for a few months. Six years, four books and three TV seasons later, we finally ran out of tales of betrayal, theft, humiliation, dishonesty, cheating, lying and nudity. We moved on, we grew up, but crucially we carried on betraying, stealing, cheating, lying and accidentally forgetting our clothes in front of royalty.

So when the Radio 2 call came, it wasn't long before the pressing need to open the doors of the national confessional again became obvious. A generation who had listened on the way to school were now doing the school run themselves. Fresh employees who listened while starting work were now running their own businesses. Humble students are now professors of nuclear physics (well there's at least one I know of). Many years and many misdemeanours later, we were ready to go again.

Some things can be confessed straight away, but many, it seems, need to hang around, to fester, to niggle away for quite a few years before the circumstances seem right for seeking forgiveness. Most of the tales in this book have now ripened to maturity and await your judgement.

On the air, it of course needs the Confessional Collective to pass judgement on a daily basis, and so my humble thanks to Sister Rebecca, Brother Matt and Sally our Mother Superior for their wisdom, dispensed so stylishly. Also for that golden moment when one of them says, 'Something like that happened to me . . .' and I know it'll be a while before the next song gets an airing.

So here it is, the latest collection of confessions; I hope you enjoy them. And if they spark a pang of guilt somewhere in your soul, you know what to do. My confessional is always open.

Families

It all starts here, of course, in the intricate and tangled web of family life. These are often the stories that take the longest to emerge; small and insignificant misdemeanours get caught up in our highly complex relationships. Rivalry, jealousy and deceit were good enough for the Bible and Shakespeare, so they'll be just fine here too.

Making a Pastry Retreat

Dear Father Mayo and the Adventurous Collective,

I am writing to seek, nay beg, forgiveness for a sin which to this day brings a tear to my eye and a lump to my throat.

It was Christmas Eve long, long ago. In fact, 1984, and I was nineteen. I had spent the late afternoon and evening in the village pubs, and it had been decreed that my mother would come to the pub at precisely 11.30 p.m. to collect my father and me in order that, as a family, we could go to midnight mass. My mother arrived at the pub and quickly diagnosed (despite not being medically trained) that I was a little the worse for wear and that instead of attending church I should go home instead.

I downed my final pint and bid goodnight to my fellow drinkers, staggered up the hill and fumbled my way into a nice warm house, which was full of the smells of Christmas. My mum had spent the day baking in preparation for the many guests who would arrive the following morning. Ah yes, the smell. I remember it well. Even a few hours after they had come out of the oven, the unmistakable aroma of mince pies still filled the air. This was a small village that didn't have a chippie, let alone a kebab shop, for traditional post-pub dining purposes, and so the waft of warm fruit and pastry called me to the kitchen. The mother of all baking tins was on the worktop, lid slightly ajar to allow the last remnants of heat to escape, and it was crammed full of freshly baked pies. Three dozen of them, in fact.

I grasped the tin and slumped to the kitchen floor, leaning against the back door. The first pie was delightful, but for a growing nineteen-year-old, it barely touched the sides, so I helped myself to another, then another. It didn't really register with me that the pies were not as filling as usual. All I knew was that every time I put my hand to my mouth there was a bite of mince pie waiting to be chewed. After a while I lazily put the cake tin on the floor and just about managed to find my feet and wander into the lounge.

In front of the chimney was the scene familiar to households up and down the land – a generous glass of brandy and a mince pie waiting to nourish Father Christmas when he stopped by our house to deliver presents. Having got a taste for mince pies, I found myself reaching down and taking Santa's and stuffing it in my mouth. The umpteenth pie took the last bit of moisture from my palate and was a little hard to swallow, so I reached for the brandy and in one gulp finished off Santa's drink.

No sooner had I finished drinking it than I felt the need to dash up the stairs to the bathroom, where I passed out.

Christmas morning came and went and so did the guests and so did Christmas dinner, the Queen's speech and indeed daylight. When I eventually staggered down the stairs it was approaching 5 p.m. I was 'greeted' in the lounge by a stern-looking father.

'You'd better apologize to your mother,' he growled.

'Why, because I missed Christmas dinner?' I piped up innocently.

'No.'

'Because I was sick on the bathroom floor?'

'No.'

'Because I was a bit too tipsy to go to church last night?'

'No.'

What awful deed had I committed? All became clear as my father explained that I had managed to ruin all thirty-six mince pies, leaving nothing for my parents to offer their guests.

There was a reason the pies had not seemed filling. It seems that each time I had taken a bite of pie, I had put it on the floor beside me while I chewed. Then, rather than finish that pie, I had reached for a new one and repeated the performance. When my parents had arrived home from the pub, they had not been greeted by the unmistakable smell of mince pies but by a nasty stench of my own making. My dad had carried me to bed and my mother had spent half an hour scrubbing the bathroom clean before going into the kitchen to discover my mincemeat and pastry carnage.

So, Father Mayo, I beg forgiveness. However, I am not begging forgiveness for getting tipsy, being sick or demolishing my mother's baking. I was nineteen and living in a very dull village with nothing better to offer than beer. What did they expect me to do? The crime for which I am begging your forgiveness is the dastardly act of consuming not only Santa's mince pie, but also his brandy. It was a cold night and he had a lot of work to do and going without his mince pie and brandy could well have been disastrous for some poor child further down the route to whom Santa did not deliver because he had run out of energy. I have probably been punished already because I have never been left any presents at my parents' house since that fateful evening, but I still ask for you to forgive me on Santa's behalf.

Kevin

What a Racket!

Dear Simon and the Collective,

I ask for forgiveness for a misdemeanour of mine committed some thirty years ago, when I was young.

I was just fifteen, living with my mum, older sister and younger brother in an old stone cottage surrounded by fields in a sleepy English village. In those days, life was far less complicated.

I was a hard-working boy and earned pocket money by cutting the grass and undertaking any odd jobs the elderly residents offered me. My money-earning was driven by my passion to own a brand new air rifle with 4×40 telescopic sight and leather shoulder-strap, the kind that boys could only dream of. The day eventually came when my total savings, along with the trade-in value of my much older model, meant the dream purchase could take place.

It was Saturday, 11 April 1981. My mum took me to the gun shop where I was allowed a few test shots and shown how to set up the telescopic sight before my dream gun was boxed and tucked under my arm. How proud I was. As soon as I got home, I took it into the back garden and continued my target practice to get the scope set up precisely before retiring to bed.

The fateful Sunday morning in question I awoke and went down to the garden, where I continued with my shooting practice and having the best time ever. By lunchtime, the shooting targets were not satisfying me any more and a greater challenge was needed.

Now, just outside our cottage in the farmer's field was a

large electricity pylon with ceramic insulation discs. These discs were occasionally subject to target practice with my old air rifle, with little or no effect other than a satisfying 'ting' as the pellet bounced off.

I turned to the electricity pylon and squeezed the trigger of my new purchase. Even before I blinked there came a huge explosion that shot fire and sparks right down the power line. Stunned, I stood there with a sick feeling in my stomach. My mum ran out the back door and said, 'We've got no power. What on earth have you done?'

I pointed to the electricity pylon. 'I shot it! But it never used to do that with my old air rifle!' With that my mum told me to go upstairs and hide the offending item. I slid it under my bed, well under. Feeling sick with fright I went out to play badminton on the front lawn with my younger brother, hoping nobody would suspect two young boys innocently playing racket sports. After an hour, an Electricity Board vehicle arrived, packed with workmen in overalls and hard hats.

Still trying to play badminton and look normal, I watched and listened to what this band of men were doing. Suddenly a voice at the bottom of the path boomed out: 'Excuse me, has anyone been shooting at this pylon?'

Very quietly, I said: 'Er, me? No.'

The angry voice said: 'We've been told by neighbours across the road that they heard air rifles being shot.'

I said, 'Well, my brother has a very old air rifle but it's only small.'

The annoyed man continued: 'Well, someone has shot at it and caused a huge inconvenience and cost. Don't expect any power for days!' With that he stormed off.

For days on end my pride and joy was hidden under my bed and I waited for the bang on the door and someone to come and take me away. Thankfully, this never happened, so I feel it is time to come clean and ask for forgiveness. And lots of it. You see, Simon, this Sunday in question, 12 April 1981, was no ordinary Sunday, but a very special one. It was the launch of the very first space shuttle, which was televised around the world to an audience of billions that very lunchtime.

You can imagine all those families, in my village and the surrounding villages, sitting down to their Sunday lunches, excited to watch history in the making, and suddenly their viewing pleasure was destroyed, breaking the hearts of hundreds of little boys who dreamed of being astronauts.

So for this mass disappointment to thousands of villagers, for dragging the entire Electricity Board out when they too should have been having Sunday lunch, and for sort of blaming my younger brother for the whole incident, I seek forgiveness. Please find it in your hearts to do so.

Tom

A Bit Teed Off

Dear Father Simon and the (hopefully) charitable Collective,

One day back in the 1970s, when I was twelve and at boarding school, I was told that the family had been invited to Granny's for lunch. Dad proposed that he and I ('the men') drive there alone in his new car, with Mum and my sisters ('the girls') to follow in the old car. I was thrilled when Dad turned up at school in a flashy Jensen Interceptor, which I hadn't seen before, and we roared off together.

I was too young to drive on the road, of course, but when we reached Granny's, Dad winked at me and asked if I would like a go. Granny lived in a fairly major 'pile' approached by a long, tree-lined drive. You can imagine my excitement at driving the powerful car slowly up the private road – though I could barely see over the steering wheel – and parking in front of the hall, which had large oak doors with the family crest depicted in ancient stained glass.

We had a splendid roast beef lunch. Then, leaving the grown-ups to finish a decent claret, my sisters and I went off to play. Granny was into golf and she said I could borrow a club and some balls and play in the grounds, but on the condition that I hit my shots *away* from the house.

Happily armed with a 6-iron and half a dozen balls, I slogged away in a very amateur fashion. I lost three balls in quick succession in the long paddock grass, then decided to return to the formal lawns and try again in a different direction. With my current poor form, I felt I was in no danger of hitting anything important, so I lined up a shot and, exactly as expected, sliced the ball into the rose garden.

However, my next shot was a corker. I middled the ball and, like a young Jack Nicklaus, gazed up in admiration as it arched high into the sky. What happened next took seconds, but felt like for ever. In horror, I watched as the ball headed straight for Dad's new car. I could barely breathe. It landed just short, bounced on the tarmac and overshot the long bonnet. Phew! But my relief was shortlived, because it bounced again and this time ploughed right through the stained-glass window, shattering the historic family image into tiny shards.

By the time I reached the door, the adults, awoken from their post-luncheon snooze, were inspecting the carnage. I knew I was done for the minute Granny said sternly, '*Henry . . .*'

'What?' I replied innocently. Despite the clear conclusion that I must have been responsible, my offending golf ball was nowhere to be seen. Unbelievably, it had rolled under the grandfather clock (from where I retrieved it later). Without hard evidence to pin it on me, the blame was eventually shifted to a possible bird strike.

I seek your forgiveness for not owning up, although I am not sure to this day that Granny was really fooled. But as she is now playing that great fairway in the sky, I cannot ease my conscience other than through supplication to your good selves.

Henry

Hammer Street of Horror

Dear Father, Mother and Children,

My story goes back to the early 1970s. I was an 18-year-old student living at home with Mum, Dad and 15-year-old brother. One evening I invited my brother to the cinema to see the film of the moment, *The Exorcist*. (Even though he was too young. How naughty of me . . .) Off we went, got our seats and settled down to an enjoyable evening's entertainment. During the scarier bits, however, I could see my brother covering his eyes. He seemed to be spooked.

Back at home my folks asked about the film and my brother tried to make out it wasn't that frightening. In the middle of that night I got up to go to the loo, and I could see that my brother, unusually, had left his door ajar and his bedside light on. So I thought I would put something to the test . . .

I took my mum's face pack and mascara from the bathroom shelf and applied them freely, waiting a few minutes for them to dry. Then, grinning hard so the face pack would crack, I checked my reflection. I have to say, it was pretty evil. I added some of my dad's Brylcreem to my longish hair to spike it out, and I looked just like Linda Blair in the head-spinning scene.

I left the bathroom, quietly crawled under my brother's bed and turned on my back. Then I started banging the bed up and down as hard and fast as I could. My brother shot bolt upright. At that moment I appeared

– head only – from under the bed, grinning manically at my now hysterical brother. He leapt out of bed, shot down the stairs, feet barely touching the treads, and out of the front door into the night, dressed only in his vest and underpants.

I should add here that he was quite a big lad who played rugby on the wing for his school, but that night he would have been picked for England if the selectors had been watching. He sprinted towards the High Street at full tilt. By now my parents were out of bed demanding to know what was going on, and I quickly explained. My father and I ran after my brother, and we were joined by a number of our neighbours who were woken by the commotion and thought they were chasing a burglar. Neighbours did that in those days. Five middle-aged men in tartan dressing gowns and slippers running down the High Street in the dead of night after a screaming youth was a sight to behold. The most surreal vision was the neighbour who joined the chase riding his ten-year-old son's pushbike and wearing his wife's pom-pom slippers.

We finally managed to reach my brother, come clean, and calm him down. To this day he hasn't forgiven me, but I would like to ask for forgiveness from the residents of this suburban town whose sleep was disturbed by my antics. Thank you.

The Evil Brother of Death from Hell

The Unwelcome Makeover

Dear Father Simon and the Collective,

My confession dates back to the early 1970s when I was a boy of nine. My parents took me and my seven-year-old kid sister – let's call her Matilda – on holiday in the north of England. One night we stayed in a decidedly posh B&B with a rather snooty landlady.

My parents were given a nice double room and Matilda and I had a room off it with bunk beds. This might not have been the best of ideas as we were always messing around and winding each other up. Mind you, in the eyes of Mum and Dad, Matilda could do no wrong. She was the golden child, and I was the naughty one. Most unfair.

Matilda had been getting on my nerves a lot that day and it was time to get her back. We were sent to bed early, ready for a prompt start the following day, and as I lay in my top bunk I became very bored and couldn't sleep. I went to the loo, and on the way back I noticed one of those dispensers stuffed with attractive leaflets brimming with holiday ideas for happy families like ourselves, so I collected a few and headed back.

After reading them all from cover to cover I was still bored, so I started to tear up one of the leaflets, as children do. The ripping noise disturbed my dozing sister, who asked what I was doing.

'I'm ripping the wallpaper,' I replied, mischievously.

'You're not, are you?' she said.

'I am, it's fun – you want to try it yourself.' And I ripped up another innocuous leaflet extolling the virtues of a working farm museum, a rugged coastal path, a mountain biking trail or a vintage steam railway – I forget which . . .

'Well, I'm going to have a go if you are,' said Matilda, and a gentle ripping noise was heard from her bunk.

'My turn,' I said, and ripped another leaflet, still safely out of her line of vision. The tearing sounds from both bunks got louder and louder throughout the night. It wasn't until the morning, however, that the devastation was revealed. The wall by my bunk was immaculate, but Matilda's had been ripped bare.

Matilda got into big trouble from Mum and Dad, who could not understand how their golden girl could have been *soooo* naughty. Worse still, we were thrown out of our lodgings in disgrace, as the landlady was, erm, very annoyed, to put it mildly. I'm afraid Matilda's halo slipped a little that night. I, on the other hand, regained my position on the pedestal.

Therefore I seek forgiveness for my crime of remaining silent throughout and letting little sis take the full rap. I also seek forgiveness from the poor landlady who had to redecorate the whole room, undoubtedly at considerable expense. Please grant me my request.

Paul

Quite A Reception

Simon,

My story goes back to the long school summer holidays of 1955 when I was a thirteen-year-old boy. I lived with my parents in what I now know to be a smart mansion block of flats in London. We had number 2, on the ground floor, and next door at number 1 lived a very smart Italian couple.

On this day my dad had gone to work and my mum to the hairdresser's. About two weeks earlier my dad had bought a new TV and had been moaning that the reception was bad, and that he must get the guy from the shop back to adjust the aerial, which was some five floors up on the roof. This was before the days of communal aerials and central heating.

With nothing better to do, I decided I would go up on to the roof myself to sort it out. I reached the roof safely, using the metal fire escape past everybody's back door. In the middle of the roof was a large chimney stack, on top of which were about ten or twelve three-foot-high clay chimney pots. Arranged around the outside of the stack were a dozen or more long metal poles with aerials on top. I could see that the one in the middle needed adjustment. I pulled myself right up on to the top of the chimney stack and perched on the edge. I could not quite reach the aerial so I put my knee on top of one of the pots and made a grab for it. I just managed to grip the end of the aerial when the chimney pot I was resting on gave way.

The clay pot, the concrete around it and several dozen

bricks disappeared down the hole that opened up beneath me. Feeling a little scared, I clambered back down unnoticed and went to see my friend up the road. Later that day, when I got back home, I heard my mother on the phone telling someone that she had returned home to find the smart Italian lady screaming hysterically in the hall, and that on going into her flat had found that a fifty-foot chimney had gone off like Vesuvius in reverse in her sitting room, covering the whole room, including her precious Venetian chandelier, hand-printed silk curtains and antique Italian furniture, in a thick layer of dirt, dust, debris and ash.

I have never told a soul about this, but now ask the nice Italian lady to forgive me, if we ever meet in Heaven.

Robert

PS That night my dad said he didn't need to phone the shop after all as the TV reception had suddenly got better.

Krafty-werk

Dear Father Simon,

I am seeking absolution for something that began around twenty-five years ago and is *still* going on.

Like many children I had an active imagination, some might say an *over*-active imagination. It is fair to say that in my salad days I told fibs. *All* the time!

My creativity was employed to particularly good effect at school. Perhaps it was an attempt to impress my friends. Back then, I came out with some whoppers. I once pretended my village had a football team called Pugstone Rangers. I also claimed to own the club, despite only being nine. I pretended to have a girlfriend living in Liverpool. Why wouldn't I? I frequently told anyone who would listen that I was the youngest qualified sword swallower in the UK and I maintained that my uncle had invented the fridge freezer.

Alas, my friends were clever for primary school children, and quickly saw through my tall tales. My ambitious claims became a source of entertainment for them, and humiliation for me. Nevertheless I persevered, giving a lurid account of Kelly McGillis coming round for tea, and declaring I owned a real-life Chewbacca and had applied to be Margaret Thatcher's milliner.

The ridicule continued and I was on the verge of calling time on my fanciful falsehoods, when I stumbled upon what would become my greatest triumph. One day we were discussing European countries, when I remembered my parents telling me they took me to Germany when I was six months old.

'I was born in Germany,' I proudly declared.

I braced myself for my friends' onslaught. I was surprised, stunned even, when everyone believed me. Not only that, but they seemed genuinely interested and eager for more information. I blurted out some spontaneous responses to their questions: Leipzig . . . Bayern Munich . . . same colours as Belgium's.

Later that week, I had a few friends visit after school. Coincidentally, my mum had some photographs out of our time in Germany – yours truly, dressed in small baby attire. My friends would occasionally grow suspicious and asked me progressively more complicated questions. But I was always one step ahead.

Why didn't I have a German passport? I was registered when we arrived in England. Why couldn't I speak German? I was too young to remember any. Why didn't I support Germany in the 1986 World Cup? I didn't fancy them after they lost to Denmark in the Group stage.

After a while, I decided to stop making up new things, but my alternative birth reality had taken on a life of its own. Simple things like taking German GCSE fuelled the fire. Over the years the subject was brought up many times, and never doubted. Controlling when to cheer and when not to at England–Germany sports fixtures was a considerable form of stress to me.

I knew there was no turning back the day I got married. Every single speech on the day made reference to my Germanic heritage, and despite the audience being full of my family, people who had known me my whole life, including my mother and father who were present at my birth – nobody batted an eyelid.

After they had finished their toast, I took my two best men to one side and told them the truth. They had mixed emotions about my true origins but they did vow to get their own back at some time in the next twenty years.

I am still awaiting that punishment. In the meantime I seek forgiveness for misleading my friends; and from their parents who still commend me on my international roots. I seek forgiveness from Kelly McGillis's friends, sword swallowers and, most of all, the whole German nation, for pretending to be one of them for so long.

Herman

Seven Seas of Why

Dear Father Simon,

. . . and the kind-hearted, beautiful people who create the confessions panel on your wonderful show. Prompted by Herman's sword-swallowing tales, I must confess to a little white lie of my own. You don't need to be a parent to know the timeless questions all children will one day ask: 'Where do babies come from?' 'Why do I have to go to school?'

Many years ago, this happened to me when my daughter, who shall be referred to hereafter as Persephone, asked me: 'Where did you and Mummy meet?' Now, on this occasion, history has no option but to show that I did, inadvertently, give the wrong answer here. The truth is that I met my wife when we both worked in a hospital, but I'd told that story thousands of times and one is always interested in impressing one's children.

'I used to be a pirate,' I said, leaving a dramatic pause for effect, and also to see if this was going to be accepted. 'And one day, while sailing the seven seas, we captured a ship and on board was a beautiful princess. Well, I made everyone walk the plank but I kept the princess as my wife.'

You know how it is, Father Simon. As parents, we respond to, literally, hundreds of millions of questions a day. Little lies can slip into an answer at any time. How was I to know this one was going to spiral catastrophically out of control?

Of course, Persephone told all her friends. 'Where's his ship?' they asked. Luckily, and almost as if someone somewhere was endorsing my lie, at that time in the city where I lived was an old trawler that had been converted into a pirate-themed restaurant, complete with Jolly Roger. So, off we went to see it.

'We had to sell it to buy a house when you were born,' I casually explained, while looking longingly at the bow of my old ship. I may also have affectionately stroked it and said something like, 'We had some good times, eh, old girl?'

This seemed to stave off further questions for a while. But kids, like all good investigative reporters, can't be kept at bay for long.

'Where's the treasure, then?'

'Buried on a secret island, of course.' (Well, where else?)

With the production of a rather believable 'ye olde map', courtesy of my brother who conveniently worked in a theatre, I was even able to show exactly where our treasure was buried. And yes, Father Simon, X did mark the spot.

We kept up this pretence for many years. I downloaded a pirate dictionary, regularly bought limes 'for old times' sake', and would laugh ostentatiously at the archaic methodology employed in *Treasure Island*. I even grew a big black beard.

Father Simon, I seek not forgiveness from Persephone, who rumbled me when she was eight, and who remembers the tale with affection. Or indeed from my many relatives and friends, who were forced – at various times – to participate in this charade. I don't even require absolution for mocking the work of the great Robert Louis Stevenson.

No, Father, I seek forgiveness from Persephone's friend, let's call her Diana – she knows who she is – who carried on believing this tale until she was *eighteen*, much to the amusement of *all* her school friends.

(Captain) Jack

Spurred On

Dear Simon and the Collective,

While listening to the recent confession by Captain Jack, who managed to convince his daughter that he was a retired pirate, my mind was taken back to a little lie I told my daughter a few years ago.

Unfortunately, compared to Captain Jack's little white lie, which snowballed, my fib was cold, calculated and downright mean.

You see, Simon, as my chosen alias would suggest, I am a big Spurs fan, and a few years ago found myself in the awkward situation of having married into a family of diehard Chelsea supporters. Twice a season, I had to take a ribbing from my extended family after my beloved team had suffered yet another defeat to our London rivals.

One autumn Saturday afternoon, I was sitting at home relaxing, watching the football results come in, while my then four-year-old daughter sat at the other end of the sofa colouring in, when she looked up at me and enquired, 'Daddy, what football team do you support?'

I told her I supported a team called Tottenham Hotspur, and her next words made my blood run cold.

'Really? I support Chelsea.'

I was horrified. The thought of the apple of my eye joining the dark side was just too much to bear, so without really thinking things through, I replied: 'Well, that's a shame because Father Christmas does not visit children who support Chelsea.' My daughter looked at me in horror, and as her eyes widened and her bottom lip began to quiver, I realized the full weight of the statement I had just made.

Simon, the natural thing to do at this point would have been to give her a hug and tell her that Daddy was only joking. But instead, to make things worse, I gave her a hug and told her not to worry as all that was required was for her to do the right thing and become a Spurs fan, and I would ring Father Christmas and tell him the good news, and she'd be back on his list.

Guilty doesn't even cut it, Simon, but over the next few weeks no more was said, so I thought my devious lie had been forgotten about, until months later, a couple of days before Christmas, when my concerned little princess checked that I had rung up St Nick to inform him she was now a Spurs fan . . .

I would like to beg forgiveness from my lovely daughter for any sleepless nights I may have caused her with this wicked lie, and from jolly old St Nick for tarnishing his clean-cut image and portraying him as a grumpy old man who discriminates against children depending on their chosen football team.

Guilty Spurs supporter

Own Goal

Simon,

I feel inspired by the soccer-related tale to come clean about my own footballing misdemeanour.

One Friday afternoon a couple of years ago, my car had broken down. I don't mind missing work, but the next day was a Saturday, match day, and my beloved, mighty, magnificent Exeter City were playing. I really needed to make that journey.

I trudged in my front door and asked my girlfriend Janet if I could borrow her car to take to the football, but the response was: 'What? Football? It's my birthday tomorrow, John. If you go to the football on my special day, I'm leaving!'

Needless to say, the rest of the evening was rather quiet at home.

The next morning, we woke late and I made Janet breakfast in bed for her birthday, subtly stuffing the personalized Exeter FC shirt I'd got her into the cupboard – judging by last night's conversation, this wasn't quite the perfect birthday present I'd imagined it to be.

I was still rather sore about being told what I could, and couldn't, do, and I was determined to see City win . . .

'I'm not going to the football but I still need to borrow the car – my dad needs my help for about an hour this afternoon,' I said.

Amazingly, she bought this, and said it was fine, as long as I was home by 2 p.m. . . . Well, I'd worry about that later.

So I zipped off to the game and watched City dismally lose. On the way home, feeling rather bitter towards my team, I was starting to regret my rashness, thinking maybe I should have stayed home on my dear girlfriend's birthday. Maybe I should have missed just one game? After all, I do like Janet quite a lot. Maybe I should just tell her I'd spent the time with another woman. Let's face it, she'd be less mad . . . but just then, passing the fields and woodlands of Devon, I saw a herd of deer and the perfect excuse sprang to mind.

I stopped the car, got out and started kicking the front wing until a large dent appeared. I flattened the seats and spread out the assorted junk in the boot into a deliberate mess. I grabbed some mud and spread it around the back. I looked down at my pristine Exeter City shirt – it had to be done – and rubbed mud all over it . . . perfect.

Upon walking in my front door hours late, I saw fire and brimstone in Janet's eyes. 'How dare you?' is the broad-castable part of what she said. But as I tried to speak, she walked out of the door, only to see her dirtied and dented car. 'What have you done now?' she yelled.

'I was trying to tell you – on the way home, I hit . . . well, I hit a deer.'

Tears welled up in animal-loving Janet's eyes.

'I'm sorry – it wasn't dead, I couldn't just leave it there! I had to take it to the vet's – then, because it belonged to the estate, I had to fill in a police report. I'm so sorry about your car, I'll clean it now.'

Her tears flowed. 'Oh, John! I am sorry.' She flung her arms round me, tears falling on my red and white stripes . . .

So I seek forgiveness for the lies told to Janet, her anguish for an imaginary deer and her car which I never fixed – the relationship didn't last long anyway, as my excuses for why I wasn't around on Saturday afternoons, bank holidays and some Tuesday evenings got more and more elaborate.

John

Always Check Your Mirrors

Dear Simon,

This story goes back to the late 1970s, when I was twenty years old, and although I have told a few people, it is still one of those moments that makes me put my head under the covers at night and go, *OH NO!*

I had been going out with a girl, let's call her Alison, for a couple of months when she passed her driving test, so she suggested that instead of going to the usual places on a Friday night, she would borrow her dad's car, pick me up and we'd go to a country pub for a meal and a drink.

The following Friday there was a knock on the door and there she was, looking great, and ready to take me out on the town. The night itself was a typical November one, cold, dark and absolutely pouring down, and as Alison wanted to talk to my sister about something she suggested I wait for her in the car. So I ran to the car and jumped in.

From my vantage point I could see Alison and my sister chatting away and I settled down to wait. However, I quickly realized that I desperately needed to break wind, which I did very loudly and with a terrible secondary effect. The car filled with the foul smell immediately and I knew that when she returned to the car she would know what had happened, and this might put a damper on the evening before it had even begun.

So I wound down the passenger window and started to fan, then scoop, air from inside the car into the cold November evening.

I could now see Alison finishing up her conversation with my sister and starting to run towards the car. Now in panic mode I was actually blowing air out of the car, but somehow I managed to get the window closed a micro-second before she opened the driver's door.

Hooray, I thought, the moment is saved, just in the nick of time!

Until, that is, Alison opened her mouth, and uttered a sentence that will live with me for the rest of my life. In a very clear, conversational tone, she said, 'Have you said hello to Mum and Dad?'

I felt my blood turn to ice. The hairs on the back of my neck stood up and I felt physically sick as I turned my head to see her mother and father, whom, incidentally, I had never met before, sitting silently on the back seat.

We drove in silence to a local church meeting where she dropped her parents off for the evening, then we went on to the pub. Alison commented a couple of times during the evening that I seemed quite distant, but I told her I didn't feel very well and we were home by 10 p.m.

Alison and I went on to marry and then divorce, and in the entire time we were together that story was never mentioned by anyone involved. Both of her parents have now passed on and I have not seen her for fifteen years, but even writing this has brought back the horror again. However, I feel a certain relief at having finally confessed.

Any chance of forgiveness?

Mike

No Place Like Home

Simon,

Going back a few years now, while my wife was pregnant with our third child, we were renting a house, our own being in the process of a massive refurb. The house we rented was of a good size, and although we were only there a short time, it was long enough for us to call it home.

Now, one Friday night in November, we decided to go to our local pub. My wife wasn't drinking, so she was driving. As the night went on, my wife grew tired and we had what to some may be a familiar conversation. It went a little like this:

'I'm tired. I think we should go.'

'Why don't you head back, and I'll follow on foot when I finish my pint?'

My wife probably knew I would consume more than the pint I was holding, but anyway she left to drive home to bed.

After one or two more drinks (I wasn't counting . . .), I started my trek home. As I reached our road, I remembered I didn't have my keys. I hoped the door would be unlocked, and to my immense relief, it was. Being the caring husband I was, I decided to crash on the sofa so as not to wake my sleeping wife. I fell asleep as soon as my head hit the pillow and I must have slept for about three hours.

When I awoke, the first thing I needed, unsurprisingly, was a glass of water. I headed to the kitchen, picked up a glass off the draining board and had a quick drink and a nibble on some nice biscuits my wife had kindly left on the worktop. By now I needed the comfort of my own bed.

Without my contact lenses everything was a little fuzzy so I started to climb the stairs on all fours, so as to be as quiet as possible. You can imagine my horror when I came face to face with a growling dog at the top of the stairs. You see, Simon, we didn't own a dog, and it was at this point that it dawned on me there were quite a few other differences too, such as the decor . . .

I was in the wrong house. In fact, I wasn't at all sure where I was. I slowly backed down the stairs, through the front door and stood for a moment outside, trying to collect myself. As I looked around, I saw the mistake I had made. There across the street stood our rented house. It would seem that in my drunken state I had walked up the wrong side of our road.

I scurried over to the correct house. As it was now morning, I was greeted by my pregnant wife with a knowing 'tut'. I started my explanation of why I never made it home, and as a result of this being only one of many situations I have found myself in over the years, she wasn't terribly surprised.

Due to our short stay left at the property, we both decided it best not to go and explain, so I beg your forgiveness for never confessing to my temporary neighbours that they had unknowingly put me up for the night, and for leaving them wondering why their sofa looked like a crinkled makeshift bed, why a half-finished glass of water was sitting on their kitchen worktop, and why their full packet of chocolate digestives was mysteriously reduced to a pathetic pile of crumbs.

Please forgive me.

Yours truly, Mr P

Meter the Action

Dearest Brother Simon and the Ecclesiastical Collective,

I would like to beg your forgiveness for a distant and dark deed that has been burning on my conscience for the past thirty years, and for which I feel I shall burn in damnation for all eternity should I not reconcile myself with this dastardly act.

It was the summer of 1980, on a council housing estate. Times were hard and there was a general need for frugality amongst families, not too different from today. My parents were struggling to keep their heads above water and both had to work full-time, leaving me and my two sisters to be latch-key kids. We were given our own errands to carry out in the evenings prior to Mum and Dad returning home from work, expecting a tidy house and an evening meal, with homework done. It would then fall to me to run to the local shop for errands for my mother, then the task list would be completed. On a Friday evening it was my job to go to the cupboard that housed the electricity and gas meters, and insert 15 × 50p coins into the electricity meter and 10 × 50p coins into the gas meter. My parents must have felt I was trustworthy enough to do this.

I remind you all that it was summer, and we were on the six-week school holidays. I was a free twelve-year-old, who enjoyed each summer day without homework. All I wanted to do was play with my collection of Action Man figures and associated tanks and helicopters. Well, Simon, it was during one Friday evening, whilst pushing in the 50p pieces, that I happened to notice the electricity meter had small bits of twisted wire attached to it, which each ran through what looked like a squashed lead blob. I twisted one of them and it came away in my hand. It looked, in the imagination of a twelve-year-old, like it could be used as a kind of hand grenade for Action Man. Indeed, so did my friends James and Johnny the very next day, who also played Action Man. They wanted some of their own, but I dared not tell them the shameful truth that our humble home harboured coin meters for our gas and electricity. I told them I didn't know where it had come from, but that evening, I looked at the meters and discovered they both had these little 'grenades' fitted all over them. I collected a grand total of sixteen of them to share out and felt that I would be, for a day at least, the best mate to my two Action Man aficionados. Sure enough, I was heralded a hero.

Some weeks later, when the meters had been emptied by the men from the electricity company and the gas company, we were all sitting enjoying our tea when two men knocked at the door. They explained they were police detectives and were following up a complaint that the meters had been tampered with. They stayed for some time talking to my dad and examining the meters, before taking him to the police station. Our mum had to catch a bus to the police station to await any further outcome.

I would like to seek the forgiveness of my dad, who was later released when the police were made aware that no money was missing and all the accounts tallied up; of my mum, who had to go and sort things out, and of my nan, who had to drive fifteen miles to sit with us while we all panicked about our dad and the possibility of him doing porridge. And from all three of them for never having the nerve to confess before today.

Phil

The Concrete and the Clay Beneath My Feet Begin to Rumble

Dear Simon,

After nearly thirty years of carrying this burden of guilt, I feel it's time to confess to a deep dark secret and solve what has remained a mystery to many people.

When I was twelve, about five weeks into the summer holidays, I started getting bored. I switched on the TV and it was the kids' show *Why Don't You*. They were demonstrating metal detecting and showing the wealth of dirty metal clumps they had found over the years.

I didn't have a metal detector, but I decided to go and dig for treasure anyway. I grabbed my dad's garden spade and an ice pick, and walked over the fields looking for somewhere to dig. I lived near a motorway then, and I ended up at a tunnel that ran directly under it, behind the houses at the top of my road. It only led to fields and nobody really used it, so it was deserted.

Underneath the northbound carriageway of the tunnel I dug for about twenty minutes until I hit something. Of course, at first, in my excitement, I thought I had found a Saxon hoard or a Roman helmet, but alas, it was just concrete. I continued to dig round it and expose more. I found it was about three feet wide and curved either side and just kept going on and on.

I got bored trying to find the beginning or the end of this thing, so I decided to throw bricks at it, hit it with the spade and then go home, leaving a slightly cracked concrete slab and an extremely large hole behind.

I forgot all about it until three months later, during a particularly cold November, when my family and I were watching *Minder* in the lounge and my mum, breaking off from the witty banter between dodgy dealer Arthur Daley and his downtrodden employee Terry, said, 'Can you hear that sound?' Well, Simon, at this point we all began to be aware of a rumble, with bangs and people shouting outside.

Going to the front of the house, my mum opened the curtains and screamed – and I really do mean she screamed – 'Mr Prendergast's shed is floating down the road!' My dad, brother and I rushed to join her and saw what can only be described as a raging river where the road should be. Simon, it was terrible, as tea-chest-sized chunks of soil, sets of matching garden furniture, branches, a greenhouse, a kid's slide and much more besides made their way down this new waterway.

Looking up the road to the houses behind which was the motorway tunnel, I saw water flowing through gardens, garages, and number 264's recently installed kitchen. At the other end of the road it was flowing straight into the new wine warehouse that had only just opened, and this, as it had been built below the level of the road, was starting to fill up alarmingly quickly.

Five hours later, after the police, fire brigade, council, water company and even the army had finally stemmed the flow, I found out that I had uncovered – and then cracked – the pipe that led to the reservoir two miles away. The force had been so great that, when it finally burst, pieces of pipe embedded themselves in the roof of the tunnel.

According to the local paper, 1.2 million gallons flooded out, while the water company still couldn't understand why it had happened. So: to the Prendergasts, Mr Parker, the Newmans, Mrs Burton and her dog, the Shahs, the Coopers, the Fergusons, the Williams and all the others, I finally beg your forgiveness.

Bill

The Dupes of Hazard

Dear Simon and the Collective,

Listening to your confessions recently, I was reminded of an incident in my past which I am quite ashamed of, but also still find a little amusing, especially when I have to use my hazard warning lights.

I have two sons, Jack and John. Many years ago I was in the fortunate position of having motor manufacturers lend me cars for evaluation, sometimes for many days at a time. Thus I found myself with my son John out in a top-of-the-range Mercedes, enjoying a trip down to see Grandma. I was trying out some of the considerable optional extras, and John was beside himself with excitement, not only because of the car but also the rare chance to ride in the front passenger seat, just him and me.

'What's this switch for?' he kept on asking. All our family are avid James Bond fans, and so my plot was set. Pressing the switch to raise the rear sun blind, I informed him this was the 'bullet-proof screen'. I was able to work the Command Centre with secrecy from the steering-wheel controls, and it was great fun telling my son we were getting secret messages from 'M'. There was also the sat-nav system, which in one mode showed a small circle with crosshairs: the targeting system for the ground-to-air missiles. The car had four heat-seeker missiles, I explained, denotable from the number of exhaust pipes. Hearing all of this, he was in a state of ecstasy, and it was then that he spotted the red triangular button in the middle of the dashboard. 'Sorry, John,' I said, putting on my serious voice. 'In no circumstance should this button ever be pressed. Not only does it launch the ejector seat, but it sets the booby-trap system which blows the car up in five seconds.'

Well, we had a great time on our visit and John had enough stories to tell not only the family but all his friends.

However, a couple of days later my little plot backfired. This time my wife Sue was at the wheel with both of our sons in the car; I was at work at the time. As Jack is older than John, he was allowed to sit in the front passenger seat on this occasion. All was well and John was instructing both my wife and Jack on the car's special features from the back seat, which was OK, until the red triangular button on the dashboard was pushed by Jack. John, horrified that his brother did not heed his warning about this forbidden feature, started screaming and crying hysterically that they were all going to die in five seconds' time, not good when you're travelling at 70 miles an hour on a motorway.

My wife had no choice but to pull over on to the hard shoulder to console John, a jabbering wreck, who shot out of the car and started running up the motorway embankment. Even the motorway police and the man from the breakdown recovery service could not entice him back. My wife got me on the phone and I was eventually able to convince John that, because of the red button's horrific capabilities, I'd had it disarmed to protect my family. It took me an hour to persuade him back into the car.

For many years, John remained nervous of the little red button on any dashboard. He would sit quietly in any car aware of where the red button was and break out into a cold sweat if anyone even moved their hand towards it. Now that John is starting to have driving lessons, it's time for me to confess, to save him from embarrassing situations with driving instructors. So I beg of you and the Collective to absolve me of my little fib, which has both shamed and amused me for the last ten years.

Martin

Driving Miss Dairy

Dear Father Simon and Reverend Team of Forgivers,

My confession relates to an incident that happened many years ago but has haunted me ever since. When I was nine my dad got a job as a milkman, and I used to help him before school and at weekends.

One day, he was offered a new round delivering milk to some posh houses in the town's affluent suburbs. For this, he was given one of the dairy's brand new sparkling milk floats. This electric marvel was magnificent. The faux-leather-padded seats were a world apart from the hard bench seat and dodgy cushion arrangement we'd had in the floats of old. I was in awe.

Early one morning, Dad proudly double-parked the float alongside a row of swanky cars in front of these resplendent Regency dwellings. Their well-kept stonework, glistening in the streetlights, was only dwarfed by the array of glittering cars parked outside. My dad took a crate of milk, headed off into a retirement home and began putting the milk outside each apartment door. Meanwhile, I had completed delivering to a few nearby houses and returned to the float. Now, I don't know if it was the fact that I was so enamoured with the new machine or if I thought my dad would be impressed, but I decided to move the float further down the road to continue deliveries while I waited for Dad to finish inside.

Well, Simon, milk floats are not complicated machines; one switch to select forward or reverse and two pedals, go and stop. What could be simpler? I sat in the big seat, ran my fingers around the shiny steering wheel, selected 'forward' and pressed the accelerator pedal to the floor. Unfortunately, having never driven anything before, I had no idea that the steering was so heavy and I just couldn't turn the wheel enough. Also, electric vehicles accelerate rather quickly when 'floored', and although the top speed was only 30mph, I found myself doing that almost immediately, as the float bounced uncontrollably off the row of posh people's cars lined up outside their splendid abodes.

One by one, the front corner of the float scraped down the sides of the cars, removing door handles and mirrors with consummate ease, before I managed to bring this awful event to a halt by finding the brake pedal.

Panicking, I put it into reverse and, gently this time, moved it back to where it had been then got out to survey the damage.

My dad returned to the float just as I finished kicking the last piece of mirror under the last damaged car and I knew I had to do the decent thing. So I began chatting casually about how I'd seen a car further up the road driving erratically. My dad peered into the gloom ahead as he drove further up the road, saying he couldn't see anything, and within seconds we were past the row of scraped cars. We finished the round and I cycled home wondering how I was going to explain myself later that evening after school.

But, Simon, nothing was mentioned, no stern-looking Dad, just his usual cheery self. The following day, however, as we got to the road in question, my dad was soon confronted by a gentleman who was gesturing towards his damaged car. I knew now the game was up, even though my dad was giving a convincing performance as someone who had no idea what the man was talking about. I was sure that when they looked at the front passenger side of the float there would be no denying it was the perpetrator of the damage, as the float had been left with some tell-tale grazes and a bent bumper end when I had inspected it the previous day. Obviously, not wanting to draw attention to the damage, I'd gone out of my way not to look at the front of our float all morning, but I knew what was coming when my dad and the man walked round to look at the float. While my dad said, 'I told you so,' and the man scratched his head in disbelief, I looked and to my amazement saw nothing but a clean, shining, undamaged corner.

My dad asked me to recount how I'd seen a car wildly speeding off and suggested that perhaps it was this driver who'd caused the damage. The man took this information on the chin and walked off, muttering about how that sort of driver should be strung up.

Returning to the dairy, Dad went to the office to cash up while I waited. Then the dairy's mechanic popped his head through the window. He asked me to tell my dad to be careful with this new float as it had taken him a whole day to repair it, but he'd kept it quiet so as not to get my dad into trouble for hitting a gatepost or lamp-post. 'Or wall?' I cheekily piped up. 'Yes, or wall,' he repeated, nodding knowingly as he walked off.

Simon, I seek forgiveness for my over-zealous belief that I could handle this vehicle, from the people whose cars I damaged in my attempt at driving the milky behemoth, from the mechanic who spent all that time unwittingly covering up my misdemeanour, but most of all from my dad for not having the 'bottle' to tell him what happened. Finally from the dairy, who were blissfully unaware, but were so nearly saddled with what would have been a hefty repair bill or insurance claim. I hope you and your venerable team can find it in your hearts to give me some solace at last.

Ashamed of Gloucestershire

Spire-elling Out of Control

Dear Father Simon and the Holy Collective,

Many times I have sat at the keyboard summoning up the courage to put my confession into words, only to back away to retain this story of deception and wickedness in the depths of my mind. The burden is too great to bear any longer; so I now pour out my soul to you.

The story involves my older sister, and my crime may have been born out of jealousy – after all, she had passed her 11-plus and gone to a prestigious grammar school, whereas I had failed and simply gone to the local comp; she'd had mentions on the Simon Mayo evening show and even won a jar of Mayo, whereas I had never had a mention at all; she even owned the 'Confessions' book, whereas I had to ask permission from her to even glance at it.

This story takes us back to the 1980s, when I was a boy of fifteen. Our parents had taken us, my two sisters and me, on holiday to one of the UK's attractive cities, known for its cathedral, a place steeped in history and holiness – and it was within the actual cathedral precinct that we were staying, its magnificent splendour only a stone's throw away.

Family holidays for fifteen-year-olds can be a difficult time for everyone. This time, tensions rose even further. You see, my older sister, let's call her Kate, was in her O-level year and had projects to do. Rather than simply let her get on with these projects herself, our parents made me and my twin sister help her. Can you believe this? On holiday, but having to help your sister with her schoolwork? This was just asking for trouble . . .

One particular piece of work was a geography project. She had chosen to investigate the distribution of visitors to the city. The plan was to question people in the street, clipboard in hand, with such gripping lines as, 'Where are you from?', and 'What are you doing here today?' To complete enough questionnaires she required help – and that's where my twin sister and I were dragged in. We were given dozens of questionnaires to complete, and then strategically placed in a busy area to question the good folk passing by.

When I was fifteen, I barely spoke to anyone, and most conversations were comprised of monosyllabic grunts. The thought of talking to complete strangers filled me with dread. It was then that I hatched my devious plan. Ensuring I wasn't spotted, I retired to a hidden bench to, in modern speak, 'massage the facts'.

Knowing a little about geography, I knew that a normal survey of this kind would find that most people would be locals, with fewer people coming from a little further away, and still fewer from other areas of the country. The results of this study should provide my sister with figures to produce a nice diagram of concentric circles, demonstrating the theory.

So I put pen to paper and started creating some people. The first few, naturally, came from the city itself – a couple shopping for shoes; a family doing their weekly supermarket shop. Fantasy. I then created a few passers-by who had come from nearby commuter towns. All made up. Having exhausted my knowledge of local place names, I moved further afield: a visitor there to see a poorly aunt – never existed; a coach party on pilgrimage to see the last resting place of a venerable saint – all in my mind.

But even this bored me. So next came a family from Sweden exploring historic Britain – dreamt up; a Texan oil tycoon searching for a lost child – a creation of my mind; and, of course, the tour party from Japan soaking up our culture and history, and eating pizza. Pure fiction.

I must admit, I was proud of my efforts. Glancing at my watch, I saw that it was time to go and meet my sister. She thanked me for my efforts. I grunted my reply, and we headed back to where we were staying.

History does not recall what mark she got, but it would have taken her considerably more time than predicted to analyse the questionnaires I submitted, and the concentric circles emanating from the city were rather messed up due to my meddling. Indeed, the results of my questionnaires would have led to recommendations that the cathedral be pulled down and replaced with a theme park and bowling alley, and the cathedral green be turned into a skate park.

I seek forgiveness from my sister and the Holy Collective for the extra head-scratching and work that my deception put her through, and from my parents, who, thinking that I had worked so hard for my sister, treated us all to a day at a theme park.

Yours, head bowed in shame, Richard

A Family A-flare

Hi Simon,

I have lived with the following secret for thirty-three years and the guilt is still as raw today as it was back then. It started on a bright and sunny day in May and it was my nephew's christening. Afterwards, the whole family went back to my mum and dad's house for a spectacular buffet.

A week before I had been shopping for some new clothes for the occasion and was particularly drawn to a pair of black 26-inch-flared trousers. On entering the shop I was even more convinced to buy them when I saw they had only one pair left in my size. I completed the purchase and strutted out of the shop with my bag swinging back and forth, thinking what a cool-looking guy I'd be at the christening.

During the 'after party' at my folks' house, my uncle and auntie had to leave early and so left a space on the drive for my dad to re-park, just behind my gran and grandpa's car. I'd recently passed my test, and so my dad threw me the keys to his pride and joy, a Vanden Plas 1500 in gleaming bronze with chrome shiny bumpers.

I gently moved the gearstick into first and began to pull in through the drive gates. It was at this point that I noticed the attractive girl who lived across the road, walking along to her house. I took the opportunity to impress her and so went a little heavy on the accelerator. I then attempted to put my foot on the brake but, feeling a sudden yank, I realized my flares were caught in the door and my leg couldn't reach the brake pedal. Well, you can imagine the rest – yes, I crashed my dad's pride and joy right into my gran and grandpa's car. I sat frozen at the scene for a while, half expecting my dad to come rushing out to berate me, but luckily he didn't.

This gave me time to think, so I reversed the car and put on the handbrake. I got out to inspect the damage. My dad's shiny bumper had lost its shine and was scratched and dented. My grandpa's car was fine apart from a little mark, which I was able to disguise by rubbing it with wet grass. I went back to join the party and shuffled off upstairs to change my trousers, making out to my relatives that they were a little too tight.

Later on, when everyone was leaving, my dad noticed his damaged car and turned to me. Quick as a flash, I said, 'Well I didn't notice that when I got into the car.' My father then said, 'Well, it must have been your uncle Jack, I've always thought his driving was erratic.' And so, Simon, for thirty-plus years my uncle Jack has been wondering why my dad never lets him park on the drive behind his car. As for the offending flares, they ended up in a charity shop, where they were displayed in the window.

Please will you forgive me for my sin, and spare a thought for my poor uncle Jack?

Derek

Best Left Unspoken

Dear Simon and Team,

It's time to confess to something that has been weighing heavily on my conscience for ten long years.

After a happy few days at the in-laws', it was time for my wife and our three sons to say goodbye to Grandma and Grandad. The car was packed to bursting and our four bikes were stacked on the rack at the back. I began the five-hour drive home, well aware that it wouldn't be long before one of my offspring would chirpily enquire, 'Are we there yet?'

Weaving through the country lanes, I noticed in the mirror that the bikes were moving about a little more than they had on the way, but reluctant to break the journey already, I pressed on. Soon we hit the motorway, and all bike-rack-related concerns evaporated as we cruised along steadily.

We weren't the only ones. The motorway was chock-a-block with countless other vehicles, forming three solid lanes of traffic that thundered along side by side, and then I noticed that the bikes seemed even more mobile in their rack than ever. But I hadn't even begun to calculate how far it might be to the next services when in horror I witnessed the bikes floating off one by one, like metallic confetti, out of their rack and into the air. I just had time to observe cars swerving in all directions before dragging my horrified eyes back to the road in front and beginning the job of carefully manoeuvring from the outside lane to the hard shoulder. 'The bikes have come off,' I yelled to my appalled family, before whipping out my mobile phone and dialling 999 – once it was safe to do so, of course.

I explained to the calm telephonist what had happened, and she promised that an officer would be dispatched. We parked on the hard shoulder as instructed, got out of the car and began to make our way back towards the site of the multiple bike escape. Thoughtfully, someone seemed to have constructed a path alongside the motorway for this very purpose.

We made an unhappy group: the children were wondering whether their precious bikes might now be scrap, crushed beneath the unforgiving wheels of some juggernaut. Their parents were not feeling much better, an unpleasant encounter with the law looming. We trudged in silence, wondering how on earth our bike rack could have so badly let us down. Traffic continued to flow smoothly, and, to my confusion and relief, no cars came past with their radiator grille wearing a bicycle.

It was a hot day, and the walk seemed to take for ever. When we reached the scene of the drama, what we saw left us barely able to believe our eyes. Instead of the expected carnage, we found our bikes leaning in a neat row against the central barrier, apparently undamaged, while the traffic continued to race noisily by as if nothing had happened. Soon a police car appeared. As the officer clambered from his vehicle, his frosty gaze swept over the marooned bikes, then me. Thinking he might be about to produce handcuffs, I babbled something about a 'bike rack malfunction', as though he should arrest the bike rack rather than me. To my relief he did not feel the need to arrest anyone. He sensibly declined to cross the carriageway to get the bikes, and talked briefly into his walkie-talkie. As is usual with such devices, I could hear clearly enough what he was saying, but the sounds that came back to him through the speaker could not be recognized as speech. However, he seemed to have no difficulty interpreting it. Glowering in my direction, he said that more help was on the way, and retired to his car.

We settled down to wait, as the minutes crawled by like hours. Then all at once it went very quiet and we saw that our side of the motorway was now deserted. Looking some distance away, we could see a single patrol car. It restrained a massive throng of now stationary traffic that rumbled and bellowed angrily beneath a thick cloud of exhaust fumes. Our officer signalled us to join him in retrieving the bikes and, with this done, he left without another word. His colleague released the traffic, which set off at a pace that suggested I had made every driver late for the single most important appointment of his or her life.

Another century passed as we tramped back to our car and I put the bikes on the rack, each one held in place by a pair of rubber clasps. The final task was to fasten two safety straps around the whole lot to make sure they couldn't break free. It was at this point that a sickening truth dawned on me: while being distracted by an argument over who was going to sit where in the car, I hadn't attached those straps earlier before we left the in-laws. Oh no! The whole grisly episode was my stupid, careless fault. Reasoning that to confess could cost me my marriage, my children or quite possibly both, I kept quiet, and from that day on I have continued to do so.

Simon, I know I did a careless thing. I know the episode taught me a lesson in safety I have never forgotten. Please find it in your collective hearts to forgive me.

David

School

The happiest days of your life, that's the theory. And that may well be true, if you go on to have a miserable life. It is inevitable, with all those teachers, all that homework and all the hormones, that this will always be a rich playground for confessions. As parents, we would rather not know what our darlings are up to because we remember very well what we were doing at the same age. Here are a few gentle reminders.

The Awkward Assembly Affair

Dear Father Simon and your worthy sidekicks,

I write to beg forgiveness for a vendetta committed by myself and my friends in the 1980s. Back then we were incarcerated in an all-girls boarding school. One particular girl in the sixth form, Gina, was very unpleasant, and foul towards all the younger girls.

After tea we were allowed to change from our uniform into our home clothes, and at this stage the torment would start. I was thirteen, rather overweight and quite spotty. I was always dressed in a sensible corduroy skirt, one of my brother's cast-off check shirts and a cardigan. Meanwhile, Gina was the epitome of fashion with gold stilettos, mini-skirts, fishnet tights, make-up and the trendiest hairstyle. Me and my friends would be made to parade through the hallway of the school while the sixth form looked on and, egged on by Gina, pointed, jeered and laughed. This sometimes reduced us to tears. We were desperate to get even.

After a few terms of this I decided to seek my revenge. We had a laundry room, where we took our dirty clothes. They would be washed and dried by matron and put back in the lockers in the basement, from where you were expected to collect them. Anything missing a name tape would be put in lost property, and at assembly on a Saturday morning the head-mistress, ably assisted by the matrons, would parade around with the unmarked items until she found the owners. Every fourth Saturday she would have the day off and the very shy, awkward assistant headmaster, Mr H, would have the task of handing out odd games socks, Aertex shirts and nighties.

I set about rallying support to bring maximum embarrassment to Gina. Over a period of days, we took it in turns to take her skimpy bras and sexy knickers out of her laundry locker, cut off the name tapes and drop them unceremoniously into the lost property basket. Presumably thinking these items had been delayed in the wash, Gina said nothing. Saturday assembly arrived. I had timed this carefully, and Mr H was on duty. At the appropriate point the lost property basket was wheeled out and you could see the horror on Mr H's face as instead of the usual odd games socks and Aertex shirts, he picked out pair after pair of skimpy undergarments.

Gina clearly wasn't prepared to let the knickers go that easily, and every time another pair was picked out she would go bright red and put her hand up to claim them. The whole school burst out laughing, wolf-whistling and jeering. Poor Mr H looked like he wished the ground would open up beneath him, and we nearly cried, we were laughing so much. The final bra was handed out and Gina fled the room in tears as we all dispersed to our lessons.

It was a silly, juvenile thing to do but it gave us poor homesick girls so much pleasure. We laughed about it for weeks, nay terms afterwards. I beg forgiveness for being as unkind to Gina as she was to us – two wrongs don't make a right – but mostly for our treatment of Mr H who, traumatized by the whole episode, left the school shortly afterwards.

AB

A Maroon (or Four!) Too Far

Dear Simon and Confessional Crew,

I feel the time has come to confess to a deed that occurred many years ago. In the late 1970s, I attended a public school in London. Afternoon activities ranged from rugby to cross-country runs, all of which seemed to involve running around in the rain and getting muddy. Being a more sensitive and artistic chap, I fully involved myself with the drama department instead. School plays were presented each term and a dedicated crew of creative individuals was needed to build and paint the sets and props and organize the lighting and sound effects. It was not very taxing, and there was ample opportunity to explore the depths and heights of the huge hall/auditorium and climb up into the roof above the stage, which gave us crew members extra kudos amongst our peers.

When the script came to the stage crew for the next production, we would pore over it and note down a list of requirements from the director's notes in italics. We were all very professional, given we were only fifteen years old. The junior play in 1978 was called *Woodhead* and I vaguely remember the plot was about the Victorians building railway tunnels across mountains up north. What I remember far more specifically was our reaction to one of the stage notes: *There is a loud explosion, lights down, end of Act I.*

There it was in black and white, the director's instruction: a *loud explosion*. We never used to pay a lot of attention to the dialogue, but on this occasion it seemed necessary. It seemed that this was a critical point in the plot. The play was about the perils that faced poorly paid Victorians working in dangerous conditions without safety gear, and this scene was to depict a young man using a pick-axe too close to poorly stored dynamite. Sparks fly from the rocks he hits with his axe and ignite the dynamite. Bang!

We looked at each other and grinned widely. Excellent!

On our trip with the drama teacher to the stage hire shop, we perused the notes we had made, and one of our team raised the subject of special effects. 'Yes, I know about the explosion – a very important part of the play,' the teacher declared from the driver's seat. 'A maroon ought to do it.'

Sure enough, after a brief discussion with the assistant in the shop, the necessary equipment was handed over. Education is a wonderful thing, and on that day we learnt the formula for a good stage explosion.

1) For the sound: a stage maroon – a little larger than a cotton reel, black with two yellow wires sticking out, it's basically an electronic banger. Wire up to the mains, flick the switch. (Came in packs of six.)

2) For extra echo: it is recommended to hang the maroon inside a plastic dustbin under the stage.

3) For the visual side of the explosion, the flash and the smoke: a teaspoon of flash powder – magnesium – heaped over a piece of low-watt fuse wire between two terminals on a small box. Switch on at the mains in sync with the maroon. (Came in a pot about the size of a mug.)

Remembering that the combination of words 'health' and 'safety' had little meaning in the 1970s, our drama teacher let us get on with all the jobs we had to do, making the judgement that we were sound-minded youths who would act correctly when given responsibility.

The set was built, I single-handedly painted the entire back wall of the stage area with a fabulous diorama of rolling hills and meadows, and we came to the dress rehearsal, which was the first time we were going to try out the explosion. The actor (a first-year called Robin) brought down his pick-axe hard on to our plywood rock face – *BANG!* It was fantastic! A large boom came from under the stage and perfectly in sync came the flash and small white mushroom of smoke, which dispersed quite quickly. Lights down, curtains swept shut, lots of applause from cast members and 'Well done, boys' was heard from the front row as the approving drama teacher looked on.

The following night was the first performance and we reassessed our explosion. Nothing wrong with the bang, but we all agreed there could be a bit more smoke from the flash device.

So that night, a second teaspoon of flash powder was added. The result was even more impressive, a packed house of proud fee-paying parents applauded wildly following the surprise and the visual impact of our end to Act I. We were on a high!

The following evening was the last night, traditionally the one when the headmaster, governors and honourable guests make up the first couple of rows in the audience, and as was normal the stage crew assembled a couple of hours before the performance to prepare for the evening.

We all agreed that the flash had been far better when more powder had been used, and decided that it seemed wasteful not to use the rest of the pot. We also had four maroons left. I can't remember whose idea it was, but, in short, they were all wired together and suspended in an empty paint can at the back of the stage about three feet from where young Robin was going to be standing.

In our defence, halfway through Act I we started having second thoughts, but there was no way we could gain access to the device as the only trap door was in the middle of the stage.

And so it was that on that night came the most phenomenal controlled stage explosion London had ever heard. Robin brought down the axe and the switch was flicked. The bang was ear-splitting, the flash seared retinas and the smoke that rose looked reminiscent of footage associated with atomic-bomb testing.

In contrast to the roar of approval from the audience on the previous night, there was a stunned silence. Because the curtains were now shut, the rising smoke had collected on the ceiling and begun returning to stage level. You could hardly see across the stage. Three floorboards had been ripped from the joists and there lay poor whimpering Robin, holding his ears. Someone peered around the curtain and confirmed that the parents had started to move slowly away in a stunned manner for refreshments. Robin was quickly carried off to the side by a couple of older boys.

'That sounded louder than last night,' said our trusting drama teacher, who had appeared in the wings.

Mark, a fifth-former, stepped forward confidently. 'It must have been the positioning of the dustbin, sir. Sorry, I didn't have time to move it to under the middle of the stage.'

There was a moment of silence (I say silence, my ears were whistling), a quizzical glance around, the floorboards were hastily replaced, and the drama teacher appeared to accept this account of events and sauntered off for a glass of wine.

Ten minutes later the curtains were opened again, releasing a huge wall of heavy white smoke that billowed on to the front rows of the audience (headmaster, governors and dignitaries). And the play was completed without further incident.

The next day there was no evidence anywhere of the paint tin under the stage floor, just the yellow wires hanging limply. Robin was pretty deaf for about three weeks but didn't appear to suffer any permanent damage, but the true under-stage firepower has never been revealed to anybody until now.

I seek forgiveness from all involved but in particular from the governors and parents who had to watch the second half of a school play through a dense fog and with their ears ringing.

Andy

The Delinquent Directors

Dear Father Simon,

I would like to bare my soul to you and your esteemed panel of moral judges in relation to an event from my youth that has troubled my conscience ever since.

It all began with a school camping trip to Hampshire. I and three of my friends, who shall for their own protection remain nameless, set off for a brisk walk in the wooded countryside.

An hour or two into our journey, one of the foggy mists this part of England is famous for started to roll in and in pretty short order settled all around us. Before we knew it, we could see no further than a metre or two ahead. Being sensible types, we started to search for a refuge, and soon found ourselves in a nice clearing with a very large wooden structure. We took shelter under the eaves of the structure and even found a load of fold-away chairs to sit on. Imagine the delight of four teenage lads when we discovered the chairs all had 'BBC' printed on their canvas backs. They looked just like director's chairs from the movies!

And so it was that we took to the clearing and began to act out all our favourite movies, with each of us taking it in turns to be the director in a 'BBC' chair. The chairs also became multi-functional props, from chariots in *Ben Hur*, aeroplanes in *The Blue Max* to horses in any number of cowboy films we could have named for you back then. Eventually we were worn out and so we sat down in the middle of the space and waited as the mist slowly lifted.

When it did, we saw that the grass we sat on, well, wasn't really grass any more. In fact, it resembled something more like a building-site access road, or a well-used rugby pitch, having been devastated by four manic boys on wooden steeds.

Father Simon, I can hardly bring myself to tell you what we

saw next. As the roof of the wooden structure materialized, so did the large sign on top of it. It said: 'Brockenhurst Bowling Club'.

We all exchanged horrified glances, quickly replaced the canvas chairs and ran as fast and as far away as we could. The incident was never mentioned again – by us, at least. I'm sure the local media, residents and particularly club members mentioned it a lot, and for many, many years (as I fear it may have been that long before their prize bowling green fully recovered).

So, can I please beg forgiveness from the local residents and the members of the club, first for trespassing on their property and using their chairs in such an irresponsible manner, secondly for turning their perfectly manicured grass into a quagmire.

Yours hopefully, Mike

The Color Purple

Dear Father Mayo,

I ask for forgiveness for an unfortunate incident that occurred during the should-have-known-better days of my early teenage-hood.

In the early 1980s I was at school in the south-east of England with my mate, whom we shall call Simon, and we were both content with attending a rural educational establishment. Our village schooling consisted of the usual mix of lessons and sporting activities, but the highlight of our week was always chemistry. Being of enquiring minds, we liked to take the more interesting lessons, learnt with a healthy enthusiasm inside the classroom, outside . . .

It is for one such instance that I seek your mercy, as with the benefit of hindsight I can now see we may have gone too far. One morning the chemistry teacher demonstrated an experiment (the purpose of which eludes me now) that showed how potassium permanganate was a powerful, purple colouring agent when mixed with water. Having learnt of the dyeing effects of this chemical, I was struck with an idea.

Why chemistry teachers leave storeroom doors unlocked and unattended, especially during breaks, is beyond me (and I'm sure nowadays this would be in breach of some health and safety regulation). Anyway, my mate and I ended up with a rather large jar of the afore-mentioned chemical.

The walk home from school was quite lengthy. However, I knew of a shortcut across someone's garden. A small stream flowed past the bottom of this and other gardens until it emerged under a bridge in the village high street. Being secluded, and obscured from general view, the garden was the ideal location to empty the contents of the purloined vessel to see for ourselves the scaled-up version of our recent education.

The crystals were poured into the stream and turned the water into an astounding deep shade of purple. Seeing the speed at which the colour spread and dis-appeared into the undergrowth downstream, I ventured that if Simon and I ran fast enough we would be able to witness the newly dyed water appear under the high-street bridge.

Sadly, we didn't win the race. When we arrived, the once glassy, pure outpouring already resembled some-thing from a psychedelic purple nightmare and continued to flow into the distance and the next village. Somewhat disappointed, Simon and I went home and thought no more about our race and the stream.

The following day two local newspapers ran the headline story of how a local resident had polluted a significant stretch of the county's waterway, as the purple contamination had been traced upstream to his back garden. There was mention of his dumping a substance, yet to be determined, in an irresponsible fashion and that the local environment police were pursuing the case.

Coupled with this, the poor chap also suffered a somewhat cold reaction from his neighbouring home-owners who had their once picturesque garden stream, populated with the odd stickleback (which now looked very odd) and a lot of riverside vegetation (which now looked even odder), deemed to be poisoned, thus lowering house values for future property buyers.

Our endeavours to further science in both water coloration and stream versus human racing instead left me feeling responsible for a home-owner getting a rough time from his neighbours, the local press and, worst of all, the local environmental protection agency and the police. Father Mayo, I seek your forgiveness.

Nigel

A Case of Progressive Pilfery

Dear Father Simon,

In the early 1970s I was in the sixth form of a grammar school in the south-east of England. Like most sixth-form boys in those days, I was heavily into prog rock, *The Lord of the Rings*, girls and writing poetry. My friends and I listened to the new albums from the likes of Pink Floyd, Genesis, Yes, etc., though my personal favourites, Emerson, Lake & Palmer, were inexplicably mocked by my schoolmates.

Being of a literary persuasion, I regularly contributed to the school magazine. Sometimes my writing was of the trendy stream-of-consciousness variety; at other times I submitted poems about matters that occupied the mind of the adolescent male (i.e. the aforementioned prog rock, *The Lord of the Rings* and girls).

Our school offered annual prizes for academic and sporting achievements, and one of these was for poetry. My ambition to be the next Ted Hughes or John Lennon was whetted by the thought of winning this prize. I decided to write a poem that would be different from all the other Tolkienesque or pastoral or teenage angst-ridden entries I knew would be offered.

Inspiration came from Curved Air, another fine prog band, whose members were the overwhelmingly gorgeous singer Sonja Kristina Linwood and, er, some blokes playing instruments. As well as doing unspeakable things to Vivaldi's *Four Seasons*, they also had a hit single around this time called 'Back Street Luv', and the sight and sound of the amazing

Ms Linwood, *in person*, belting out this track when I saw the band at our local civic centre gave me my cunning idea.

It was based on the assumption that old fogies like the masters at the school, some of whom were forty or even older, would never have heard of Curved Air, let alone any of their songs.

And so it was that I began my opus – I remember some of it to this day. It started: 'Summer's coming, time to dream the day away, and he's so funny is the boy who came away.' This may have had some loose and subconscious connection with the beginning of 'Back Street Luv', which began: 'Summer's coming, time to dream the day away, and she's so sunny is the girl you met today.' And so it continued until I had finished changing a few words here and there (but only a few) in Sonja Kristina's wonderful song.

Well, Simon, not only did I win the coveted shiny Poetry Cup, but I was highly commended for being so imaginative and for telling such an inventive story. In addition, the poem was published in the school magazine, and I was photographed holding the trophy aloft on the front cover. I was extremely fortunate that no one thought to inform any of the teachers that my work wasn't entirely original – a downright rip-off, in fact.

So I now seek forgiveness for such bare-faced plagiarism; for deceiving the teachers and the boys who had never heard of Curved Air into thinking this was an entirely original poem; for having the nerve to collect my prize at a ceremony where I was applauded by the entire school, teaching staff, parents and visiting Important Guest Speaker (whoever that was); and most of all from the ever-gorgeous Sonja Kristina, for shamelessly using her song to achieve my selfish ends.

I await your decision . . .

John

Exam Cheat

Hello Simon and Team,

I listen to your confessions, and I now feel I would like to be absolved of a blemish on *my* character. I am sixty-one and enough time has elapsed for me now to confess my guilt.

During the final year at my boys' school the students undertook exams in several subjects. Those who were successful were awarded the School Certificate. The school promoted the Certificate, and many an apprenticeship was gained by the holder. But the standards needed to achieve the status of 'Certificate holder' were particularly high.

Our form teacher, whom I'll call Mr Roper, was also our history teacher and therefore set our exam paper. He was as old and as boring as the subject he preached on. Hardly the most motivational of educators, he often told us we were no good and would never pass the Certificate.

One day, shortly before our exams, he excused himself from our history class and, unusually, did not lock his desk as he left. I immediately clocked this situation. I was worried about the subject, full as it was with dates and times, in one decade and out the other, so to speak. So, Simon, I took it upon myself to go to the front of the class and look inside his desk (an act that those days would surely result in the cane if caught). There before my very own eyes, like a chest full of glistening treasure, was our exam paper. I had struck gold.

With one eye on the door, in case he returned suddenly, I read out the questions to my eager audience – and let me tell you, Simon, in the whole year of the history syllabus, I had never known them so silent or attentive. I then replaced the paper in the desk, closed the lid, quickly returned to my seat, and the whole class was looking quietly studious when Mr Roper came back into the classroom.

Well, the outcome was that everybody passed, some with distinction. The school had never known such splendid results, and Mr Roper was complimented by the Head and the educational authorities on the high quality of his teaching. No one grassed me up; if they had, I would surely have been expelled.

Simon and friends, I ask for your forgiveness please for putting thirty students out into industry, which mistakenly thought they were good at intake and retention of information. More importantly, they set off in life in possession of the much sought-after School Certificate which they did not deserve in the slightest, some of them going on to become captains of industry, and have careers as MPs and judges, and other lofty positions.

I now beg your pardon.

Robert

Long-distance Lorry Skiver

Hi Simon and the Team,

The events confessed here took place in the mid-1970s when I was at school in a leafy suburb close to an English city.

It was rather a stuck-up institution that liked to make its pupils play 'rugger', which was fine if you were a huge brute who had reached puberty early but total misery if, like me, you lagged slightly in the physical development department.

Head of recruiting cannon fodder for the first team to practise charging at was a terrifying, hairy chemistry teacher we'll call Mike Jones. He was constantly press-ganging me into the firing line as I was in his set for chemistry (which I also lagged behind in).

Towards the end of a particularly cold and rainy season, he collared me once again to play in a vital match. I blurted out the first lie that came into my head. 'I'm sorry, sir, but I am unavailable as I have to compete in the cross country.' The 'Cock House Run', as it was known, was scheduled for the same afternoon.

This ruse had seemed like a good idea at the time but unfortunately Mr Jones consulted the head in charge of cross country – let's call him Bruce Garner – who was an equally terrifying six-foot-five geography teacher. He was only too pleased to have an unexpected volunteer, and so I found myself plodding reluctantly round the local country lanes in the freezing drizzle.

My old chum Rich had been cajoled into the same race and we were chatting away at the back, trailing the rest of the field by some distance, when we came across a council truck stranded in deep mud in a ford. It was the sort with a cab at the front and an open pick-up section behind. The driver was at the wheel while his mate pushed, unsuccessfully, at the rear.

Quick as a flash I saw the opportunity for a break from the tedious run. 'Do you need a hand?' I cheerily asked. Rich wasn't too keen, but with three of us heaving away from behind we soon managed to get the vehicle back on to the tarmac ready to go. As the council worker climbed back into the cab a brilliant wheeze struck me. 'May we just cadge a bit of a lift from you please?' I enquired. Of course, they were only too glad to return a favour, so I climbed up on to the open back section with the reluctant Rich. After a few directions to the driver we were soon sailing past the other runners, laughing and waving some 'cheery gestures' as we went. The looks on their faces were a picture that remains with me to this day.

Once we had passed the leaders we asked the driver to drop us off and, in the interests of fair play, stood to one side as all the competitors dashed past before joining the race to finish in joint last place.

Our innocent little jape harmed no one and did not affect the all-important Cock House scoreboard. Unfortunately someone grassed us up. We were hauled before Mr Garner and given a right old rollicking – dangerous behaviour, disrespect to venerated school tradition, lying to get out of rugby . . . We were ordered to do 'defaulters' in the quad for a week.

I seek forgiveness, not from Rich for getting him into trouble, nor from the other runners, but from the other more responsible members of our house, as my actions tarnished our house's reputation and gained us no extra points – just embarrassment. I would also like to beg forgiveness from Mr Garner and Mr Jones as I went on to become a teacher and now realize, through bitter experience, what an irritating little git I must have been to them.

Regards, Paul

A Straight Flush

Dear Simon and the kindly Collective,

Some seventeen years ago I was still in secondary school. I was a very good student – I almost feel able to use the word 'model', in fact – and I was always polite to both my fellow students and the staff. I was also known as a bit of a boffin.

While some of the things we did in science lessons appalled me – dissections, for example – others enthralled me. In one of our lessons we were shown how a particular chemical exploded when in contact with water – demonstrated by our teacher under controlled conditions, of course, then repeated on a much smaller scale by us students. My friends and I decided we wanted to try out a little more than the minuscule amount we'd been allowed in class. Being the trusted well-behaved boffins we were, we weren't being watched as closely as the slightly more energetic students, and thus we managed to pocket a rather large amount of the chemical between us. Later we headed for the toilets intent on our experiment, but we had second thoughts. We imagined the damage that might ensue and a decision was made to return the chemical.

I retained a piece. Just out of scientific curiosity, you understand.

Later on that day I set about my lone experimentation. I slipped away from my peers during break, dropped the chemical into a toilet, flushed it and ran. The results were quite spectacular. Even before I had time to vacate the WC area, the chemical reacted with the water and exploded back up through the toilet bowl, producing a large fountain of water. The same pipe connected the whole row of toilets, and my act of flushing had driven the chemical into the main pipe before the first reaction took place, and so it was that I then witnessed an almost identical blow-back sequence in the entire row of toilets, flooding the block and making a lot of mess.

At the same time I was doing this, one of my classmates, Jane, who was well known for truanting, was doing just that: truanting. However, she had been in science with us earlier in the day and therefore became the most likely suspect. I, meanwhile, managed to depart the scene in timely fashion.

I couldn't bear to let my parents down and tarnish my lovely record so when questioned I denied all involvement. Jane denied all involvement too, but having been in lots of trouble before, she was not believed. She ended up being suspended from school for three months.

I wish now, through you, to apologize to Jane for what was an unfair suspension; to the headmaster, who got so very cross about the whole thing; to the chemistry teacher, who got into trouble for allowing chemicals out of the lab, and to the janitors who had to clean it all up.

Please, all, I hope you can see your way to forgive me.

Robyn

Parking Mad

Dear Collective,

My confession relates to an incident in 1990. Being the oldest in my year at school meant I was the first to pass my driving test, and so for a while I was in possession of a unique skill. Thus, one lunchtime, when my friend said, 'Guess what, Mum parked the car outside school today on her way to work and I have the spare key – let's go!', four of us dived into the car and had a very jolly time cruising the local streets. We returned just before afternoon lessons started.

Then we discovered the flaw in our thinking. Not only had the original parking space in the street gone, but so had *all* of the spaces. If we parked the car on a different street we would be rumbled. I had a moment of inspiration.

Leaving the car running and double parked, I abandoned the others, ran into the physics lesson I was due in and pleaded for the rest of the class to follow me. The teacher, Mr Butcher, had not yet arrived, and so most of them came.

Well, Simon, fifteen minutes of hard work enabled twenty-five sixth-formers to push enough cars in the street bumper to bumper to create a space exactly where the car had originally been. Then a quick 1-2-3 lift and we got the Astra into its old and now very snug spot.

At that point we ran breathlessly back to double physics to find a somewhat irate teacher asking why we were all ten minutes late. Luckily the few geeks who had remained in the class – out of fear, or perhaps a love of physics – had covered for us and a code of silence resulted in Mr Butcher giving up his fruitless interrogation quickly.

Three hours passed and the end of the day arrived and as we filed out of the school gates we realized the full enormity of our prank – police cars, irate drivers and tow trucks filled the road as confused drivers tried to work out how to get their cars, wedged bumper to bumper, out.

I would like to apologize to all those drivers who were stuck for some considerable time freeing their cars, especially my friend's mum, who it turned out got held up for more than ninety minutes. Her car, being the middle one, was one of the last to be freed. I would also like to apologize to Mr Butcher, who coped admirably in the face of twenty-five silent teenagers.

After twenty years, I now place myself at your mercy.

Steve

Put A Stop To This

Dear Simon and Brothers and Sisters of the Confessional Box,

My confession relates to an incident a few years back when I was an awkward teenager, sleepily stumbling towards GCSEs and battling daily with the awful hierarchy that many unfortunate children experience: the School Bus.

Initially I caught the 417 bus, which went only to my school. Being the grand age of sixteen and having proved my mettle as a bus regular throughout the years, I fared quite well. A place was usually reserved for me on the back seat and I was safe from being strangled by my tie. So School Bus life was good.

Sadly, I didn't qualify for a free bus pass, on the basis that I lived under three miles from school. As a result of overcrowding on the 417, all pupils without a bus pass were told to get the 418, which took a different route via another school in the town. For unknown reasons the two schools were sworn enemies and had been since time began. We were about to enter into enemy territory.

One morning, while our lucky chums travelled on the normal bus, I waited at the bus stop with my sister and two other unlucky souls for the 418. It arrived, we got on and were relieved to see that it was empty. Not too bad.

We drove for ten minutes with no sign of the pupils from the rival school. Just as we were breathing a sigh of relief, the bus turned a corner and there they were: forty or so enemy kids at a bus stop, pushing each other and shouting at passing cars. A grim proposition indeed.

We looked at each other in panic, but it was too late, we were well and truly cornered. A loud-mouthed blonde girl spotted us first. She called a few expletives in greeting, which was followed by a general inspection of our bags and persons by the rest of her 'crew'. We were christened with inventive nicknames, mainly based on how we looked, and were then kicked out of our seats to stand in the aisle. How humiliating. Twenty long minutes later we disembarked at school, still alive but slightly shaken.

For four gruelling weeks the 'friendly banter' on the dreaded 418 continued. Bacon sandwiches were thrown, hair was pulled and a football-style chant (not repeatable here) was even created in our honour and shouted at us daily by our tormentors. We plotted all types of revenge that never led anywhere – until one day . . .

. . . one cold and miserable day, the bus arrived at our stop as usual, but this time with a new driver who wasn't entirely sure of the route. As we got closer to what we had dubbed 'Satan's bus stop', an idea hit me. The night before, on the way home, the kids from the rival school had been boasting about their long-awaited trip to an amusement park the next day and, sure enough, there they were, waiting at the bus stop in their own clothes instead of uniform – an exciting day out ahead of them, devoid of any actual education.

With my most responsible-looking face on, I informed the inexperienced bus driver that he didn't need to stop there. When he asked if I was sure, I said I was quite sure, those kids were taking a coach today, and so we drove on past, their perplexed faces watching us go by.

I later discovered that these children subsequently arrived so late at their school that the one and only coach to the amusement park had left without them. Instead of a day out, all they got was a good soaking at the bus stop in the rain. We, meanwhile, managed to find another route into school. We didn't dare get on the 418 ever again.

I am now seeking forgiveness from all the rival schoolkids who were deprived of the fun of the roller-coaster rides, especially from those who caught colds from being left out in the rain; from my sister and friends for risking their skins in such a reckless manner, and lastly from the poor driver, who no doubt got into trouble on his first day of work for not picking up any passengers.

Yours grovellingly, Daisy

Absent Minded

Dear Simon and the Assembled Collective,

I throw myself at your forgiveness for an event that happened during my youth.

At primary school I had a certain reputation for playing pranks, of which I was proud. Whenever something went wrong, I was the first suspect. The first day at my new school arrived, and as everyone will know, the transition from primary to secondary school is a tricky one. I'd gone from big fish in a small pond to tiddler in an ocean. As such, I decided it would be impossible to maintain my reputation as prankster.

Or so I thought. We were put into classrooms, and our class was told the teacher was running late. We were also told to behave and stay quiet while they sorted out the other groups. Well, as you will have guessed, we didn't. Oh no. The classroom rang with voices and activity. On the desk there was a register. I walked over to it and, for reasons that still elude me, Simon, I opened it.

Inside were our names neatly written in black pen, but what caught my devilish eye was a gap. Clearly this class was a pupil short. I reached for a pen and wrote the name 'Snipkins' in the space.

Only seconds after this the teacher strode in and ushered us to our desks. He began reading out the register. At 'Snipkins', I replied loud and clear, 'Here, sir!' My classmates stared at me, but the teacher didn't notice I had answered twice.

Over the next few months the prank continued. All my classmates took it in turns to be 'Snipkins'. Then one day we went on a school trip to a museum. At the end of the visit, the teacher responsible did a head count and found he was one pupil short. 'Snipkins' was nowhere to be found. Terribly worried, he ran back into the museum in a real fluster and rounded up as many staff as possible.

For an hour teams of museum staff searched, along with the perplexed and panicked teacher, but of course nobody could find 'Snipkins'. At this point I had no option but to own up.

I faced the wrath of the headmaster at the time and was in detention for what seemed like weeks, but I still seek forgiveness from all the museum staff, who searched for an imaginary person, and from the teacher, who was made to look an utter fool in front of them.

Anon

Out of Pocket

Dear Reverend Pastor Simon, Monsignor Matt, Mother Superior and Sister of Mercy Rebecca,

I thank you for the opportunity to confess to an incident that has troubled me for years, and I hope the Holy Collective will find themselves able to forgive an otherwise largely blameless member of the flock.

My schooldays were spent at a prestigious (or so it thought) institution, dedicated to turning out the best minds for the benefit of the country. To its credit they did succeed once in a blue moon.

The school's ideals may have been high but we pupils were not as susceptible to the improvement of our minds as they would have liked. The majority of the pupils in my year made it safely through to sitting A-levels. With exams coming up, we really should have been studying hard, but study can be wearisome and our free periods and lunches often found us behaving, frankly, like schoolchildren. In particular, the male pupils started a craze of dispensing 'wedgies' to each other.

The wedgie – for the sake of the innocent Mother Superior – is the action whereby a perpetrator approaches the innocent party, takes hold of their undergarments from behind and pulls them steadily upwards.

This activity developed to the point where every boy in the year was targeted; however, we were fair, so this included the bookworms, the sports stars, the thin ones and the brick outhouses. Furthermore, it reached a level where not only would wedgies be given but the aim became to actually remove the undergarments from the victim. Indeed a trophy wall was started in the common room where everyone who had succeeded could pin the garments up for display.

Everyone took part, and therefore everyone was set to be a target, and thus eventually my day came. I realized the only way I could save myself was not to be a passive victim but rather, as soon as I saw them approach, reach out and quickly target someone else.

Therefore, as soon as the crowd got close, I carried out my plan, and when the mob realized that 'Darren', the innocent third party, showed more promise of yielding a new set of trophy boxers than me, he was targeted instead. I can smugly say that my plan worked and it was Darren who got wedgied that day.

But, Simon, I have more to confess. As part of the school's prestigious self-image, all pupils were required to wear a blazer, especially in the corridors between classes. The blazers had pockets which would be used to carry all manner of things. Unfortunately, they weren't terribly good at holding stuff in, and things would tend to fall out if you moved about too much. During my near-wedgie, I, like a good pupil, had been wearing my blazer, and when every-thing was over I noticed that some odds and ends (bits of paper, pencils, etc.) had fallen out of my pockets. I gathered them off the floor and stuffed everything back in.

Later on, when I reached into my pocket for something or other, I realized I'd picked up a couple of pages belonging to someone else. On giving them a cursory glance, I crum-pled them up and threw them into the bin.

Now, this happened to be the day before the deadline for university applications. These were the days when applications were handwritten and posted to UCAS. Yes, this was before the newfangled method of applying online was introduced.

Later on, I wandered past the school office and overheard a boy whimpering. At first I assumed it was the unfortunate Darren, who had gone to complain about the loss of his pants. But it wasn't. It was Crispin, swot of the highest order and head boy. He'd lost his application form to UCAS. It was too late to get a new one and as a result he wouldn't be able to apply to university that year. I suddenly realized that the rogue pages I had picked up and subsequently binned had in fact been Crispin's application.

Therefore Crispin became one of that year's exceptions and didn't go to university but instead – to the shame of his snooty parents – had to look for a temporary job to fill the time until he could apply again.

And so I seek forgiveness from the Collective for ruining Crispin's promising education, and for letting the innocent Darren take a wedgie with my name on it.

Derek

Bags of Fun

Dear Father Simon and the Evangelical Hosts,

Hearing the recent confession regarding the wonderful art of wedgies took me back to a similar pants-themed incident, for which I have carried the guilt (and mental scarring) for far too long.

The incident took place back in the 1980s, which I would suggest was a more innocent age, with schoolboys maturing at a decidedly slower rate than the headlong gallop that seems to be the norm today. Now, the nature of this confession might lead the assembled holy throng to believe the scene of the crime was some privileged private school. In fact, it was one of the UK's comprehensives, a heady mix of social classes and widely ranging academic abilities.

This incident took place during a PE lesson, a time when the obligatory black shorts, white vests and regulation black pumps gave us an opportunity to indulge in one of our favourite pastimes. Debagging involved sneaking up behind the victim, grabbing on to each side of his shorts and giving a sharp tug. The resulting sight of a fourteen-year-old resplendent in his best undergarments was itself highly amusing, but even better, as the shorts reached the ankles, was the invariable comedic pratfall to the ground.

After a particularly sprightly session of football, marked by several debagging incidents, started on this occasion by yours truly, we all trudged wearily back for the post-PE ablutions. One of our party was a lad who went by the name of 'Boggy'. He had been the victim on a couple of occasions and, walking into the changing rooms, decided it was time for revenge. He sneaked up to the nearest boy who had his back to him and, with a triumphant cry, pulled his shorts swiftly and pretty expertly to the floor. Textbook stuff. A classic 'debagging'. It was only then that we, and more importantly Boggy, realized this wasn't a boy at all, but our Religious Education teacher, who was standing in for an absent PE teacher. The look of incredulity on Mr I's bearded face as he stood with his 'trollies' round his ankles was a sight that neither I nor the other witnesses will ever forget.

As the immortal words, 'What on earth do you think you are doing, boy?' erupted through Mr I's beard (I think it was compulsory for RE teachers to sport beards), the volume of laughter from forty or so schoolboys had to be heard to be believed. Boggy was sent to the head teacher to receive his punishment, while Mr I fished for his shorts and tried to maintain (failing miserably) a semblance of dignity.

So, Father Simon, for instigating the proceedings that led to the 'ultimate debagging', I ask forgiveness, not only from Boggy, but also from Mr I, who, as you might imagine, never fully recovered the little authority he had enjoyed prior to this 'incident'.

Yours in penitence, Mr T

Snow Swearing Please

Simon,

In the early 1960s I attended a girls' grammar school in the north of England. The school was a large and ornate Victorian building. At the back the windows overlooked eight tennis courts laid out along the length of the building; there was a central divide, giving four courts in each section. It being midwinter, all the nets had been taken down.

On one particular day I met my best friend at the bus stop earlier than usual. I cannot now remember why we decided to go to school early, or even why we decided to walk, as about eight inches of new snow had fallen overnight. This amount of snow didn't seemed unusual to us back then and schools never shut because of snow in those days. Well, ours didn't. Those were also the days when only farmers wore wellies. Certainly, fashion-conscious albeit geeky and uniform-wearing twelve-year-old girls did not wear wellies.

We got to school too early to get in so, frostbite notwithstanding, we went around the back and were confronted with eight tennis courts covered in almost a foot of virgin snow – not a mark, not even an animal print on them. It was immediately obvious to both of us what should be done in this situation. We linked arms and proceeded to walk up and down the courts and write swear words in the snow. Each letter was the size of one tennis court – two swear words, four letters each – you can figure it out. We were only impeded by the fact that one of our words was not really that bad, and we'd never actually heard of one word we could have used (*Lady Chatterley's Lover*, although published in the UK in 1960, had not exactly made it into the school library). I remember we had one particular problem in that we had to do a huge long jump between letters so they wouldn't join together. We wanted capitals for our masterpiece, not cursive, you see.

Mission accomplished, we snuck into the basement to lie on some pipes to hide and thaw out before going into assembly.

Assembly used to last for ever but on that morning, the last before the start of the Christmas break, it took an eternity. A lot of neck-craning, sniggering and whispering by those girls closest to the windows, together with the absence from assembly of the four or five male teachers in our school, revealed (to a mixture of our horror and amusement) that the ancient caretaker and all the male teachers had gone outside and were wading in the snow up and down the tennis courts trying to obliterate our handiwork with their own footprints.

My friend and I were never caught. With hindsight I realize we were too geeky and too nondescript to fall under suspicion. Several older girls of the cigarette-smoking-with-attitude variety were hauled into the headmistress's office for questioning and got detention, but we never owned up. In fact, we thought we were just the biggest comedians the world had ever seen.

So I beg forgiveness of our lovely old caretaker, though I doubt he's in a position any longer to give it, of our male teachers for the half hour or so they spent up to their knees in snow, and of the girls who took the rap for us.

Yours guiltily, Louise

A Drain on Resources

Dear Father Mayo and the Collective,

As I have now just passed my sixty-fifth birthday, I feel it is time to beg your forgiveness for a misdemeanour I was responsible for when I was sixteen. At the time I was at a boarding school in the south of England. During the course of my studies I had become very interested in the sciences, in particular chemistry. I spent many hours in the school library reading chemistry textbooks, noting with interest all the exciting experiments.

I worked hard to build a good relationship with the chemistry teacher and as a result he would let me have the laboratory keys at the weekends so I could perform experiments on my own, unsupervised. I don't think that would ever happen today. (In fact, I'm not sure it should have happened then.)

On this Saturday morning I decided I would produce the gas hydrogen sulphide. This gas is actually poisonous, more so than hydrogen cyanide, but because it has such a powerful and unpleasant smell (detectable in less than one part in one thousand million), it usually does not cause anyone a problem because you *very quickly* move away. The aroma itself is like rotten eggs; it is commonly produced in small quantities within our own bodies and escapes from time to time via a downward route – thus we all know and recognize the smell!

It is made by mixing iron filings with sulphur and igniting the concoction. The result is a clinker-type substance, iron sulphide, which you add to a beaker of concentrated hydrochloric acid. The gas then bubbles out copiously.

On the day in question the experiment worked much better than I'd expected and the smell soon became overwhelming. I quickly opened all the large ceiling windows, the door and other windows, but I soon realized I had to get rid of the still fast-reacting stuff producing this awful gas and in a moment of ill-advised panic I flushed it down the sink. I ran the water for many minutes afterwards to ensure it got well down into the drains.

I then left the lab for a couple of hours and when I returned the smell didn't seem too bad, so I closed all the widows, locked up and went away to carry on with my normal weekend activities.

The next day, however, Sunday, everyone was talking about the awful smell around the school. It was the main topic of conversation. I, of course, kept my mouth shut. No one could work out where it was coming from but wherever you were in the grounds, it was there. The problem was eventually tracked down to the drains and first thing on Monday morning the water board were called to come and put things right. They sent two large vans and a number of employees to inspect the drains and they spent the whole day on the job.

So now, nearly half a century later, I beg forgiveness for the unpleasantness the whole school experienced that weekend, the problems I caused to the school administration and the cost to the water authorities. In mitigation I should mention that I did go on to Loughborough University where I gained a degree in industrial chemistry, so my experimentation was not for nothing. And, fortunately, I was never implicated, so I continued to enjoy the use of the laboratory at weekends. As a result, there are other incidents for which I also ought to ask for forgiveness . . .

But I think they should probably wait. I'm not sure the world is ready for all my admissions . . . particularly my production of nitrogen triiodide, more explosive than nitroglycerine and so unstable it will explode when a fly lands on it. Something I proved in front of a friend, who watched the final fatal demonstration with me (fatal from the fly's point of view, you understand).

I hope you can see your way to granting me absolution.

My best wishes to you all, Cliff

Top of the Class

Dear Father Simon,

After thirty years, I feel the need to unburden myself.

It was a hot, dry, still, sunny day (these details will be important later) in June, and I was stuck in a double geography lesson in a warm and stuffy classroom. Our teacher, let's call him Mr T, was passionate about his subject, although sadly unable to transfer his enthusiasm to a room full of twelve-year-old boys.

After half an hour of inattention, messing about and general tomfoolery, myself and three others were banished from the class for the rest of the lesson – result! Our prison for the hour or so left was a storeroom across the corridor, and although it had a window it was quite narrow with long shelves all the way up one wall. After staring out of the window for a while, boredom once again set in. I decided to investigate the contents of the shelves. There was nothing of any interest on the lower shelves, but on the top shelf I could see a large glass case with some sort of scientific instruments inside. I worked out that I could climb up by putting one foot on each shelf and the other on the opposite wall. My classmates were not interested in this diversion so I climbed on alone.

On reaching the top shelf, I was able to examine the glass case in detail. It was a large object, some two feet long and eighteen inches wide, and contained two drums covered in graph paper slowly rotating, with a number of fine needles moving round the drums and drawing, effectively, straight lines around each. By bracing myself between the wall and the shelf I was able to free my hands and remove the top of the case to get a closer look.

Proud of my discovery, I called down to my partners in crime, who encouraged me enthusiastically from the safety of the floor. Having taken the top off, I decided to see what would happen if I flicked the needles. Wayhay! Squiggly lines! I carried on doing this for quite a while until the novelty value wore off, then I replaced the top and climbed back down to await the end of the lesson, a stern telling-off from Mr T, and lunch.

We had assembly at school every morning, a chore to be endured before lessons started. However, the next morning, the format was a little different. There was Mr T up on the stage, obviously in a state of some excitement, accompanied by an overhead projector with slides showing blow-up pictures of graph paper with squiggly lines on it.

Once we were all settled he launched into an excitable account of how there had been some unprecedented meteorological activity the day before, measured by the school's technical equipment, normally associated with an anticyclonic front and extreme weather, even though the previous day had been still and dry. He then went on to postulate a theory, based on late-night study, that this type of phenomenon – although unusual in hot and dry weather – was not impossible. The headmaster thanked him for the interesting presentation and told us that the local paper would be in school later on to interview Mr T and take some pictures so we were all to be on our best behaviour.

The story was published in that evening's paper, together with a picture of a grinning Mr T holding up some graph paper with squiggly lines on it. There was also a rumour of a call being made to a world-renowned geographical magazine.

I now seek forgiveness, not for the ensuing embarrassment to Mr T when the truth came out – as it did a couple of days later – because he was a small-minded, mean man and I believe he deserved everything he got, but for the punishment my classmates received for a crime that was entirely mine.

Naughty Schoolboy

Work

If anyone was still remotely interested in class war, I could have arranged these as workers' and bosses' confessions. There is still, however, clearly a 'them and us' tension. Sometimes this can lead to a strike and other times to a confession. Occasionally, as you will read, these tales spill over into romance, revenge or the 'I'm so knuckle-chewingly bored I'd do anything to stay alive' section. But here's an insight into the British workplace in all its glory.

Rude VDU

Dear Simon,

I was a geek even back in the 1970s and it was my geekiness that led to the events for which I now seek absolution.

I went to a university that was next door to a museum, and one of the exhibits there was a computer game. Back in the 1970s these were very rare and so well worthy of a display in a museum.

The game was a simple one. The computer asked you questions, trying to guess the name of an animal you had previously thought of. You typed the answers using a keyboard and a green glowing VDU. All very innocent stuff. Fun for all the family.

Being a geek I tried the game out too but on one occasion, when I played particularly poorly, I did something very bad. I typed a rude word into the terminal. It immediately shut down, presumably, I thought, because some clever programmer had ensured that it would.

On Wednesday afternoons, us geeks were allowed to 'play' in the computer lab at the university. What we quickly realized was the computer in the museum next door was actually the university's computer (so rare and expensive were they at the time).

We also worked out that if someone had written the program that detected rude words, somewhere in the university computer in the lab there had to be a list of these offending words, which would be a jolly fine and funny thing to find and read.

After several Wednesday afternoons searching, we found the list. I am now a respectable man in my fifties, and I can tell you there were words on that list I still don't know the meaning of and I can only assume were very rude indeed.

We thought it would be a jolly wheeze to print out the list, in large font, of course, to show to our friends (and of course for further research). Choosing our moment carefully, my accomplice stood by a very large noisy printer that printed on to large sheets of green and white striped paper, and I issued the command.

We waited and waited. Nothing happened. The printer remained silent and inactive. We walked up and down the lab, thinking things were not normally that slow. In the end we realized it was not going to happen. Then it dawned on us. If the set of rude words had not appeared on the printer and they had been sent somewhere, where had they gone?

Well, turning up at the lab the next morning there was a noticeable 'atmosphere'. Apparently the words had been sent to the VDU in the museum next door, where several visitors, expecting a simple innocent game of 'Guess the Animal', had been shocked to see a stream of disgusting words pass in front of them.

The university authorities, not unsurprisingly, were very upset, but fortunately we covered our tracks enough never to have been caught. But for many years it has weighed heavily on me that it could have been a child who had seen these words and it may have had a detrimental effect on his or her upbringing.

Over thirty years on, it's now time to seek absolution. It was, after all, an accident. And from it I learnt my lesson. Without this I might have gone on to a life of international hacking crime, rather than pastel-coloured spreadsheets in a small office in the country.

Please forgive me.

Geeky Trev

It's An Ill Wind That Blows

Dear Father Simon and the Collective,

My confession goes back to the far-off days of 1990 when petrol was 40p a litre and I was still a student. I had managed through a friend of my father to get a summer job working for a local bakery as a handyman, somewhere in the south of England.

One of my jobs was to drive round all the small satellite stores in my Mini Clubman to service those blue-tubed insect electrocuters, replacing the tubes and cleaning out the trays full of sparked-out insect parts.

In the middle of the summer with the windows down, the stereo blasting and no boss to watch over me while raking in £5 an hour and 25p a mile (at 40p a litre a pretty good profit), and of course able to drive down pedestrian high streets and chat up shop girls, I was as happy as Larry.

On a particularly hot day I arrived at one of the small high street stores to service its machine. It was so hot that the pair of revolving ceiling fans were at full speed doing their best to keep air moving in the stuffy shop. I carefully disconnected the unit from the wall so I could take it to the back of the shop to do the service out of the way of all the cream cakes, pastries, buns, pies, etc.

Now what happened next may seem very obvious with the benefit of hindsight, but in my defence it was all about the critical timing between the circulation of the fan and me taking the insectocuter down from the wall.

As you've probably already guessed, at the precise

moment I moved the insectocuter from the wall, the strong fan swung round and blew the entire collection of wings, legs and small desiccated bodies from the tray up into the air. Looking around in horror, I saw that neither the shop manager nor her assistant had noticed the insect rain. I now had a clear choice to fess up or not to fess up to my crime.

Briefly dwelling on this issue, while still in slight shock, I noticed that it was the sticky Danish pastries that were in the main drop zone as the legs, wings and bodies gracefully fell from the sky and stuck to the sugary coating. As the shower subsided, I realized that alongside the raisins and other sticky gloss, the additional insect detritus really wasn't that noticeable.

Reasoning that the odds were in favour of not being found out provided I got the machine back on the wall before the midday rush, I went to the back room, cleaned the unit in record time and quickly replaced it. I then flew out of the shop at high speed with a cheery, 'No time to wait, got another five to do today.'

In my defence I would like to say that what I added was surely no worse than regularly happened in the main bakery and probably was of little Health & Safety risk to the people who ate the affected pastries. None the less, I would like to ask for forgiveness from anybody who bought an added-protein baked snack that day, and from the manager if she got any customer complaints as a result of my actions.

Yours sincerely, James

What Goes Around Comes Around

Dear Father Mayo,

About twenty-five years ago, while serving as a police detective, I purchased a new home. During the purchasing process I was told by the previous owners that a member of a famous pop group had once owned and lived in the property.

I was familiar with the group, who had a worldwide hit that is still played on Radio 2, but I had never heard of the individual member concerned.

Not long after moving in, I began to receive royalty cheques for very small amounts of money for this individual. Having no forwarding address, I put them to one side while deciding what to do. A month or so later I received a very large royalty cheque, worth thousands of pounds, as well as notification from a building society concerning a 'dormant' account that contained a great deal of money.

I felt I must now act and so, through contacts at my local radio station, I managed to get a message to the performer in question. Soon afterwards I received a call from his wife. She was a charming lady who was very grateful for my attempts to get in contact and happily provided me with their new address as long as I promised never to pass it on to anybody else.

The next morning, before I had a chance to send the cheques, I was called away on a major investigation and it was a number of days before I returned home. Soon after I got back, rather tired and ready for an evening of relaxation, I received a telephone call from the band member himself. He was not at all pleasant and rather rudely and arrogantly demanded to know why he had not yet received his cheques. I was annoyed by this, but I let it pass, apologized and the next day sent off the cheques.

A few months later I received another letter addressed to the householder, this time from none other than the Inland Revenue. They were writing to request information and the current postal address of the pop star, if it was known.

It only took me a few seconds to decide what to do about that.

I gathered pen and paper and proceeded to write back as if I was the musician himself. I explained that I had been away for an extended period on a very successful world tour which had also been highly profitable, and because of that and the fact that I now also had a massive chart hit, I realized I owed them a lot of money.

I asked politely if they could please calculate the total amount owing, which I would help them with should they require details, and then send me a final statement for the last two tax years to my new address, which of course I helpfully included at the bottom of the letter.

I have now retired from the police force and over the years have developed some feelings of guilt over what I did. I must admit to a pang of conscience whenever one of the band's songs is played on Radio 2, and I now feel the time has come to ask for forgiveness for my actions.

Peter

The Seaside Bus Trip

Dear Simon,

Many years ago I joined the fire brigade with a semi-automatic bus driving licence. A colleague on the same watch also had a manual licence and was driving regularly for a local company for a bit of extra cash. He came to me one March and asked if I would help him out with a pensioner trip to Eastbourne. He would drive the coach and I would drive the double-decker. I readily agreed as I needed the money; a fireman's pay was pretty low.

We set off and duly arrived after several hours' drive at our appointed destination. The two coach parties split up and arranged to meet back at the coach park later in the day, but for one reason or another we never did.

The non-stop humour and barrels of beer consumed barely offset the miserable rain that swept Eastbourne all day till the sun set. My lot were certainly fairly well oiled when I finally managed to steer them, the staggering grey nomads, back to a now deserted coach park. On the way we passed a bench where an old man lay snoring his head off. One of my party said, "Ere that's old Eric from Stokes Lane, I bet they've gone without 'im!'

Not wanting to spoil his day, we lifted the slumbering old man into the bus and on to the back seat of the lower deck, where he slept all the way home.

We all agreed to get Eric home first so I took the

double-decker right up to his door and we helped him up the path. We rang the doorbell for some time but failed to get an answer so we searched his pockets and found a front door key. Lifting a now stirring Eric carefully on to his front room couch, we put a blanket over him, left the fire on and closed the front door behind us.

As we walked down the path, a window opened in a neighbour's house. A voice from out of the dark shouted, 'You won't find anybody in, Eric and Peggy are in Eastbourne for a fortnight!'

Forgive me, Simon. Well, how was I to know? I'm off to Arabia now for a year to let the dust settle.

Edward the Confessor

Aisle Bat First

Dear Father Simon, Mother Superior and other members of the forgiveness fiesta,

In the mid-1990s, I was a fresh-faced graduate who had just embarked on a promising career in retail, for a well-known supermarket chain in the Midlands. I was working as store manager as part of a training scheme that would, in due course, see me rise to the exalted position of district manager. My normal daily tasks required me to be there at 4.30 a.m. to start preparing the store: unpack the fresh fruit and vegetables, put all the dairy products into the fridges, prepare the tills and make sure the aisles were clean and clear ready for the customers' trolleys. At 8.30 a.m., the doors were opened, I'd wish our customers a good morning and disappear to the staff room. My reward for getting through the dark morning hours was a 30-minute breakfast break once the store was primed. After breakfast, I'd return to the shop floor and make sure everything continued to run smoothly.

And this particular day was no different. I arrived at the shop, completed my normal tasks and sat down to my usual cup of breakfast tea while my team looked after the customers. And then the phone rang. One of my afternoon staff was unwell and wouldn't be able to come in. The phone rang again – another person sick. I was in trouble, as I was almost without an afternoon crew.

After fruitless checking with the morning crew to see if any could stay, I was presented with two choices: close, or jump on the tills and leave the shop floor to manage itself. Easy choice really and, being very familiar with the system, I was capable. And so I stayed on the tills for the entire after-noon, serving customers, while my shop floor slowly emptied itself of stock and floors became muddied with foot-prints. Simon, frankly, it was a mess, but it wasn't my fault.

Then matters got worse. My boss – let's call him Tony – arrived on a surprise visit, hoping to see one of his star graduate recruits in charge of a well-managed store. On reflection, though, what he likely saw was his manager chat-ting to customers on the tills while the shop looked like it had been raided. He was furious. Really furious. When the shop closed, I was given the biggest dressing-down I have ever had. I tried to explain about staff sickness, but Tony was having none of it. He issued a warning: 'I'm back tomorrow morning at 8 a.m. and this store had better be looking perfect. We'll do a store audit too and see if you've been managing the place properly.' Dejected, I went to the staff room and considered the long night ahead. One staff member, let's call him Phil, offered to help – such a kind gesture.

Well, Simon, the first few hours went well and the store started to look pretty shipshape, so Phil and I took a break for dinner and, this being a supermarket, we were presented with many options. We chose a curry from the fridge, picked up a four-pack from the beer section and retired to the staff room. I don't remember the exact sequence of events over the following few hours, but having reviewed the store CCTV tapes I can confirm that many more four-packs of beers mysteriously disappeared from the shelves that evening. So too did nearly three hundred apples, a dozen or so tins of various items and a frying pan from the cookery section. Yes, Simon (shakes head with a little shame and some pride), according to the CCTV, as the beer took hold,

Phil and I played a good hour of cricket in the supermarket aisles, using fruit and tins as balls and a frying pan as a bat. I can sadly confirm that we had an absolutely brilliant time before retiring to the staff room for water, headache tablets and sleep.

The next morning we woke and set about hiding all evidence of our nocturnal cricket – throwing fruit, tins, cans and frying pans into the waste – and completing our final checks ready for Tony to review and audit the store. At 8 o'clock he arrived and remarked on how brilliant everything was looking and, on noticing our tired eyes and unshaven faces, praised me and Phil for our dedication to the store, the town and the company. He was truly mystified by the audit, however, noting the strange range of items, from curry to apples, from tinned tomatoes to frying pan, that were missing from the store, and duly concluded that some head office administrator was likely to blame for a dodgy audit system.

I seek forgiveness here on a number of counts. From Tony, the boss, for my deceit. From Phil, my assistant, for a wicked yorker bowled right at his ankles with a tin of pineapple. From the good people of that town who couldn't buy apples that morning. And finally from the head office administrator, who probably got a kicking for a dodgy audit system.

Yours, Mark

Red Light Spells Danger

Dear Reverend Father Simon, Pastor Matt, Sister Rebecca and the especially forgiving Mother Superior,

In a previous occupation I had the pleasure of working for a local transport authority. I was based in a command centre in one of our country's larger cities. My job was a simple one – to maintain traffic flow in the area and provide information to the public.

Most of the traffic control was carried out through the use of traffic lights, the sequence of which was carefully timed to within a split-second to ensure traffic flowed as smoothly as possible. There was also a manual override to allow the operators to *finesse* the system in a way that computers just aren't able to.

As part of the service, we would also provide information to that most revered of all public broadcasters, the traffic reporter. I would routinely pick up the phone to these beautiful people and, after checking with the control room, I would update them on the current situation so they could inform their gorgeous listeners which naughty roads were best to avoid that day.

One day, I answered the call and as I relayed some very ordinary information, my mind wandered to my own journey home. I thought how much better it would be if there were no other cars to keep me company. Before I knew what was happening, I had announced there was quite a nasty jam on my route home and the area was probably best avoided and that *everyone* should seek an alternative route.

Sure enough I heard the information broadcast on the radio, and when I left work shortly afterwards, my journey home was much quieter than usual.

From that point on, whenever I needed to get back a bit earlier, I would embellish my update to the good, kind-hearted traffic reporters and subsequently whizz home. However, sin takes its toll and when I couldn't take the guilt any more I confessed all to one of the senior operators in my office. I told him how it had started, how I only used it when absolutely necessary and how I was racked with regret. My manager raised his hand to stop me speaking. My fear turned to exultation when he told me that he and another guy often did the same thing! They even enquired if I ever had a go at changing the traffic-light sequences, as that really did clear the roads.

It reached a peak one day when all three of the 'fake traffic jam' team were working together. One of the other staff members in the office suffered a suspected broken finger. Traffic was particularly bad that day and the hospital was on the other side of town so they were in for a long, uncomfortable journey. We knew what we had to do.

The casualty and his appointed driver hopped in a vehicle and we set to work. Any traffic reporters who called were told of a bad traffic jam on the route between the hospital and our office, and the lights were sequenced so they were mostly set on green for the length of the journey.

On their return to the office, both casualty and designated driver revealed how puzzled they were by how light the traffic had been. So much so, it felt like travelling in the middle of the night. However, there can be no light without shade. Traffic elsewhere that day suffered terribly. Commuters filled alternative rat-runs on their way home, confounded by reports of traffic jams absolutely everywhere and perplexed by unusually long waits at red signals.

And so I seek forgiveness from the Holy Collective, partly for my very occasional easier journeys; but mainly for the particularly shocking traffic the honest folk of the city were subjected to that day. As it turned out, my colleague hadn't even broken his finger. It was only slightly bruised.

Jake

Omni-busted

Dear Father Simon, and Brother and Sisters of Absolution,

In 1981, I was an eager-to-please if playful apprentice in a coach and bus building company in southern England. A mere seventeen-year-old boy, I was brim full of enthusiasm, not just for the exquisitely crafted feats of mobile magic we produced, but also for the dizzying array of machinery, buttons, knobs and levers I got to press, twist and pull as we nurtured each jalopy through the production process.

These machines were great showpieces of my adopted art, and each would receive the painstaking application of a hand-painted livery before purring happily from our care to their new home. As a novice (and frankly useless) member of the crew, my role during the application of this final coat was to carefully muster all I had learned so far and, armed with this knowledge, stay well away from the new bus. I was, unsurprisingly, good at this part, and watched patiently as seven expert men, my new colleagues, spent five days carefully applying the gleaming green top coat to the new vehicle.

On the final, very hot day, as the finishing touches were being made, the garage doors were closed to prevent little flies or other insects from disturbing the glass-like sheen of the glistening coach as the paintwork was dried. Finally my colleagues stood back to review their gleaming handiwork and, with a happy sigh, nodded to each other and started to pack their things and leave for the day.

This, Father Simon, is when the deadly sin of curiosity overtook my young soul, for, unsatisfied with the 52-seat shiny mass of buttons, gears, levers and lights before me, I had my eye on a new, smaller machine that crouched, winking like a mechanized minx, in the corner of the work-shop.

This machine was a credit to its kind. It had pipes; it had valves; it had dials; it had a huge hose and, most excitingly of all, a pristine, shiny trigger. At this stage I had no idea what the little temptress did, but I had to find out.

Perhaps it was enthusiasm for my new craft, perhaps it was the fumes that swirled around trapped in the workshop, or perhaps I just liked buttons. In any event my willpower (and common sense) deserted me and I walked over to the machine and flicked on the power switch, causing a satisfying growl as a powerful compressor leapt into action. I proudly grasped the nozzle and, aiming high, I drew in a breath and briefly pressed the trigger as hard as I could.

I will never forget the next few seconds. A loud hissing sound was emitted by the machine and I was filled with a mix of excitement, wonder and then utter panic as the function of my new toy became clear – it was a pneumatic grease gun . . .

Arcing high into the air like a shimmering phoenix flew a full double-axle dose (six gallons, to be precise) of top quality axle grease. The machine was a marvel of technology, dispensing the exact amount of the indelible, sticky substance directly from its spout at high velocity. As you know, Simon, what goes up must come down (a point I had neglected to consider before starting my experiment) and I quickly went cold as the output of the 'greaser' started to fall from the sky, straight towards the result of 280 hours of careful man-labour – namely the new bus.

I watched in horror as the substance seemed to multiply into hundreds of individual streams of continuous brown gloop and one by one they landed with a loud 'SPLAT' on the newly completed masterpiece in the centre of the room, leaving almost no area of the 52-seater untouched. The grease slid slowly down its shiny sides, producing a finish more like that of a camouflage desert vehicle or a safari park tour coach than a local bus.

There was really no way out of this one, and so I did what any thinking man and guilty apprentice would do and sprinted all the way home. I spent a full week off 'sick' to contemplate what I had learnt from the day. News came by post that my apprenticeship was to be completed early and I never did return to that particular workshop.

I now seek absolution, first from my employer, not just for the sick leave, but also for the fact that in a third of a second I had cost them three times my own salary in damage . . . not to mention the cost of the man-hours needed to right my misdemeanour, and the six gallons of axle grease I wasted. Secondly, from my seven former colleagues, who had to strip and repaint the whole thing over the next two weeks. Thirdly, Father, I seek absolution from the day-trippers of southern England, who endured substandard travel on inferior buses for the fortnight it took to complete the extra work.

I hope you can find it in your hearts to forgive the inquisitive youth I was by absolving the honest man I have become.

The Apprentice

The Sting in the Tale

Dear Father Mayo,

I am a pest controller in the south of England. I offer builders a same-day service for the treatment of wasps and hornets so they can get on with their work without the risk of being stung. One particularly busy summer I had a couple of builders who failed to pay, leaving me having to chase them for money – a frustrating and time-consuming chore during our peak period.

I also, of course, dealt with other pests. At a particular firm where my job was to remove an infestation of mice, normal banter had been exchanged with the builders on site – 'Surely big men like you can't be afraid of a few squeaky little mice?', you can imagine the sort of thing. Anyway, I couldn't resist the temptation to leave a live one in their van! A Jack Russell that travelled with them did catch it eventually. Not surprisingly, my name was mud in the texts I received after that incident.

About two months later, I had a call from . . . let's call him 'Bob' the Builder. 'Mark,' he said, 'we have a wasps' nest here, could you come and treat it?' A little nervous, remembering my mouse prank, I agreed, and said I would do it that evening. Bob said, 'Just leave the invoice behind the site radio and I will get a cheque to you in the post.' With no one on site, it being well after 7 p.m., I approached the job with care, suspecting revenge . . . but amazingly there was no sign of anything. So I treated the nest, filled out the invoice, placed it behind the radio as arranged and then, *Snap*! They had put one of 'my' leftover mousetraps behind the radio and, yes, it hurt a lot. I cursed them with the kind of words that can barely be repeated in public, and left, muttering to myself they had better pay up or else. At that point I wasn't sure what 'else' would be.

A week later and there was no sign of payment, so I phoned Bob, who was more concerned that I had found my mousetrap. 'Yes, no problem,' I said, trying not to think of the pain, which was still making me wince, 'but what about the cheque in the post?'

'Oh yes, I'll do that today,' he said.

Two days went by, and still no cheque. On the third day I found a hornets' nest in an old person's loft. I removed it, being the Good Samaritan that I am. This was my last job of the day and I was on my way home with the offending hornets' nest, wondering what to do with it, when I just happened to drive past Bob the Builder's site. My fingers gave a faint twinge, then I remembered the unpaid bill. Stealthily parking my car at Bob's yard, my plan to get him back was hatched.

Like all good builders, Bob had a Portaloo, which struck me as an ideal place to put this nest heaving with angry hornets. 'Revenge is mine,' I murmured, leaving the nest – about the size of a rugby ball – in the toilet. Being a responsible pest controller I, of course, was wearing a beekeeper's suit, keeping me safe from being horribly stung by any one of the many hundreds of striped buzzing beasts.

The following morning I was returning home after walking my dogs when my neighbour stopped me and handed over a letter, saying he had been away for a couple of days and this had been delivered to him by mistake. It was for me, and it was payment from Bob the Builder. Not only that, but he had put in an extra fiver for me, for providing such a prompt service.

Well, the guilt was terrible and I immediately reached for my mobile phone to call and warn Bob of what I had done in his portable toilet, and that I would be around to remove it within the hour. But just as I reached for my phone, it rang. I recognized the builders' office number. I was tempted to let it go to answerphone, but I thought, no, I will answer it, as he might not have found the nest yet. The voice was Bob's and I could hear panic in his voice. 'Mark,' he gasped, 'you will never guess what someone has done, kids most likely' – his words were actually a lot stronger than this – 'they've put a hornets' nest in our Portaloo and Jack has been stung about four times!'

'Oh my God!' was my reply. 'Is he OK?'

'Yes, but he's gone to hospital and I would appreciate it if you could get out here as soon as possible.'

'Yes, of course,' I said.

So I set off, a little nervous that they suspected me, but on arriving there, it was soon obvious that they did not . . . in fact, they revered me as their saviour. I asked how Jack was and they said he was OK but in a lot of pain. Racked with guilt, I put on my beekeeper's suit and removed the nest.

'How much do I owe you for coming out so early and promptly?' asked Bob.

After a small pause I replied, 'Normal rate, mate,' with a smile on my face.

He handed me payment immediately, saying, 'No problem, plus there's an extra tenner for being a mate and getting here so soon. I will let Jack know you asked after him. I really appreciate it.'

I have told no one of my deed, nor of taking payment for removing the hornets' nest I put in the Portaloo in the first place. The guilt has been horrendous for nearly two years now. I seek, no, I *need* forgiveness. First for my mischief, then for the deadly sin of greed! I ask, no, *beg* for forgiveness on bended knee.

Regards, Mark – A Pest Controller

Time Waits for Snowman

Padre Simon,

After many years I have plucked up the courage to face up to my misdeeds, and I humbly beg forgiveness from yourself and your wise council.

Many years ago I was a serving member of the RAF on an airfield in England. On one very cold winter's morning, all flying operations ceased – our station had been subject to a heavy snowfall overnight. That morning dawned to the sound of military snowplough engines as a valiant attempt was made to clear the runways to allow flying operations to begin. Obviously, as this was happening, the powers-that-be were not happy to see all their airmen slacking, sitting around and drinking copious amounts of tea, so we were soon dispatched out into the cold with shovels to clear the paths around our hangar and hut.

I, along with my forever-to-be-unnamed colleague, had been given the task of clearing pathways around the back of the hangar. To keep warm we set to with a flourish and had soon cleared our allocated area, but we knew if we returned to the squadron tea bar we would be sent out again. Therefore we decided, in the best traditions of skiving, to build a large snowman with the colossal pile of snow we had accumulated during our clearing efforts.

If I do say so myself, the man-sized snowman we built was a masterpiece, such that when our sergeant (a dour individual) saw the results of our efforts, he did not issue the customary and traditional rollicking for our skiving, but, amazingly, gave us a cursory nod of approval. In fact, over the course of the day we were inundated with positive comments and pats on the back for our efforts from staff on all levels.

Next morning, arriving at work in similar sub-zero conditions, we discovered to our horror that our magnificent snowman had been cruelly destroyed, its sorry remains lying flat across our newly cleared pathway. On examination it became obvious, evidenced by tell-tale tyre tracks, that some time during the night someone had run over our icy masterpiece in a vehicle and destroyed it. They had then reversed back over it just to be sure, so, Simon, this was no accident.

We were distraught, but we vowed to ourselves that we would not be defeated by this blatant slaying of our beautiful snowman, so in a matter of a few hours, and with plenty of fresh snow available, the equally impressive Snowman Mk 2 had been constructed a few metres away from the site of Snowman Mk 1.

Next morning dawned. As we arrived at work, the first thing we saw was Snowman Mk 2 scattered across the pathway. The evidence of tyre tracks made it obvious that the heinous snowman assassin had been busy at his dastardly work again.

Were we downhearted? Were we defeated? No way! Therefore, in a short period of time, Snowman Mk 3 had risen phoenix-like from the ashes, just a few metres from the site of Snowman Mk 2. But this time there was a crucial difference in our design, as, to give Snowman Mk 3 a real lifelike backbone, we carefully built him round a large and very solid, reinforced concrete bollard. Next morning could not come soon enough, and on arrival we dashed to examine him. Alas, he had also gone to Snowman Heaven, but he had obviously gone down fighting, as evidenced by a very badly damaged and bent bollard, surrounded by a sad pile of discoloured snow. Later that day we heard that two RAF policemen (who, ironically, are known in the RAF as snowdrops because of their white-topped caps, but that's by the by) were both in serious trouble after sustaining terminal damage to their service vehicle whilst larking about in the snow. I understood this cost them a seriously large fine, several bruises and minor cuts, and some indelible, career-stalling black marks on their service records.

Meanwhile, all enquiries as to the identities of the people who built Snowman Mk 3 were met with blank faces and denials from both ourselves and all our squadron comrades. Faced with a wall of silence, the hierarchy eventually abandoned all hope of discovering the culprits. I myself left the service many years later, and was seen off with a medal for long service and, ahem, good conduct.

I ask for forgiveness from both you, Padre, and your benevolent assistants, not for what happened to the despicable snowmen assassination squad, but for absolution from the overburdened taxpayers of this great nation, who due to our single-minded determination to seek revenge, were landed with an immense bill covering the cost of replacing what was probably a perfectly good, serviceable Land Rover with many years of life left in it, the cost of replacing the terminally damaged bollard, and the undoubted cost of all the military proceedings.

I bow my head and await your judgement!

Steven

Taking a Career Brake

Dear Father Simon and collected confessional professionals,

My confession goes back to the early 1980s, when I was a newly appointed, bright and keen lecturer in a college in Scotland. I was teaching a broad range of subjects to students who were – by and large – pleasant, able and dedicated. I had heard stories from some of the more experienced staff about the 'students from hell' they sometimes had to teach, and how these students would make their lives a misery for the whole year. Never having had a student like this, I put these stories down to the usual exaggeration and attempts to scare me because I was a 'newbie'.

Imagine my surprise, then, when 'John' joined my new intake the following year. John was certainly the 'student from hell' and made my life a misery. He was disruptive in class, wound up the others, missed lectures, didn't submit coursework, was quite aggressive to me if challenged and – not to put too fine a point on it – was as thick as two short planks. I tried to make the best of the situation, mindful that the chance of John passing his exams was pretty small and that as a result he would be off the course before too long.

As part of one of my courses, we had a field trip organized to Edinburgh. This was always a high point of the term, a bit of a jaunt for the students and me, getting us out of the classroom for the day. This particular year our trip was even more special because the college had – that very week – taken delivery of a brand new minibus. Indeed, our trip would be its first outing.

We met as usual at the college, feeling excited about the

new minibus – oh, aren't the seats nice, much better than the old one! The drive to Edinburgh was pretty uneventful, with me behind the wheel and my students trying to ignore John, who was being his usual obnoxious and uneducated self. My mind wandered to the exams the following week, and my delight at the thought that John would no doubt get the lowest marks ever recorded.

We parked up in Edinburgh and set out on a short walk to our destination. I walked along, bouncing the keys to the new bus in my hand. Then I heard a scream. I turned just in time to see the bus begin to roll and gather speed down the hill I had parked on – I had obviously forgotten to put the handbrake on. The bus was one day old – how would I explain this to my boss? At that exact moment John rushed past me, grabbing the keys from my hand, and ran straight to where I had parked the bus. With what can only be described as a superhuman effort, he ran alongside it, opened the door, jumped in and pulled on the handbrake. The bus came quickly to a stop, no damage done and no harm done.

As you can imagine, my 'student from hell' suddenly went up in my estimation. I thanked him profusely and (for the price of a round of drinks) convinced my students not to mention the incident to others (especially my boss) back at college.

The following week, however, I was left with a moral dilemma. I had marked the exams and, as expected, John had not scored highly. Now I could remove him from my class with impunity. He had, however, saved my bacon at a time when my other students had just stood open-mouthed. Faced with this dilemma, and full of appreciation for a job (my job) saved, I did what any moral and upstanding citizen would do, and doctored John's marks so that he passed.

John was so delighted (and no doubt amazed) that he decided not to come back the following year and got himself a job instead. I would like to seek forgiveness for my actions as follows. From the other students, who had to put up with obnoxious John for the remainder of the session. From my college (and employers) for committing the cardinal sin of falsifying exam results. And finally from John's employers who thought they were getting a qualified member of staff but instead ended up with an uneducated buffoon.

Can you find it in your hearts to forgive?

Martin

PS What has really weighed on my mind about this last part is that John left college with his exam passes and got a job in the nuclear power industry.

Down In One

Simon,

Several years ago I was the bar manager of a rugby club. I was proud of the way the bar was run, especially how clean it was kept and how good a quality the drink was. In my six years as a manager, there had never been a complaint; the excellent service was taken for granted by the members of the club.

The club was due to go on a bank holiday tour to the Midlands, and I agreed to open the bar first thing in the morning for a champagne breakfast.

At 8 a.m. sharp the drinks were flowing freely as round after round of beer was served in the cleanest of clean pint glasses. The beer was in great condition and the pints sparkled on the bar as they were gratefully received by the players in preparation for their long coach trip.

Then the club captain produced three bottles of tequila and asked me to produce thirty shot glasses for the team to drink a toast. This threw me slightly as I had not seen a shot glass in the club for several years. The bar sold mostly pints, half pints and the occasional Scotch whisky.

I was annoyed that I could not meet my obligations. I had always prided myself on my attention to detail, but now I was going to let everyone down. However, a sudden memory of some small boxes on the top shelf of the cellar came to mind. I found the boxes and indeed they contained shot glasses – enough for the job. Ideal. Or so I thought.

I rushed to the bar, quickly lined up the glasses and in

Tom Cruise fashion poured the tequila into each one in such a professional manner that no one realized there had been a delay.

The first player picked up the shot of tequila and with great surprise and excitement shouted, 'I've got it, I've got it!' and downed it in one go. 'I've heard of this tequila,' he said, 'the one with the maggot in – is it Mexican?'

'What?' I said and, looking down, realized the dusty boxes housing the shot glasses were infested with dead flies and maggots, and that each glass had a maggot or two in it. Well, I was shocked, and in a state of panic I said, 'Er, yes, that's right, it's Mexican . . . it's famous.'

'Where did you get this stuff from? I've heard of it but thought it was an urban legend . . . can you get me a bottle when I come back from the tour?' said a delighted player number 2, also downing a maggot-infested tequila, cheered on with glee by his twenty-nine mates as I stood there in shock.

Well, their coach arrived and the players left, the shot glasses were dispatched to a very efficient glass washer and the boxes were put deep into a nearby public bin to cover my tracks.

I hope the Forgiveness Collective will understand that I needed to keep up my standards for my regulars and, besides, all the bad tummies were blamed on some chicken they had at their hotel.

Am I forgiven?

John

PS *Arriba!*

The Guilty Driver

Dear Simon and the Collective,

I recently retired as a head teacher of a small but perfectly formed faith school in the north of England. As part of my duties it fell to me to run the school minibus to both pick up and deposit pupils who lived some distance from the school. The vehicle in question was adorned with lettering identifying the school and a contact number.

After a long hot day during the summer term I was driving thirteen hot and noisy pupils home. I was approaching some traffic lights and decided to pull out into the middle lane to go round a stalled van. Unfortunately, a small car with two ladies in it had decided to overtake me at the same time – so they were forced into the outside lane, which meant they had to make an involuntary right turn.

The gasp from the pupils in the bus drew my attention to the near miss, as well as the fact that the car had swerved back into the correct lane and was now in hot pursuit. I reduced speed, and as the car went past a certain amount of gesticulating was undertaken by the driver, who disappeared into the distance. Obviously I pretended to ignore it, in spite of one of the pupils observing: 'She wasn't happy with you, sir, was she?'

The following day I went into school and as part of my usual routine checked the answering machine in the office. I was treated to a blistering message from the irate driver of the previous day, which called into question not only my competence as driver but also my fitness to be in charge of children and, after about five minutes, called for my dismissal as a member of the staff of a faith school.

The caller then failed to disconnect her mobile phone, and the two ladies – obviously still in the car, having made the call immediately after the incident – continued to discuss at great length faith schools and the type of person allowed to work there and the worst excesses of religion, until the memory capacity of the answering machine was used up.

What was I to do? Not only was I the driver of the bus, but I was also the head teacher. How could I rectify the situation without compromising my position and the good name of the school, which of course was clearly written on the side of the minibus?

I went into the loo for a moment of quiet contemplation and decided there was only one course of action. Standing in front of the mirror, I firmly berated my reflection for my careless lack of attention and informed myself that I took the matter most seriously.

I then phoned the lady in question and introduced myself as the head teacher. I explained that I took this sort of thing very seriously and had immediately identified and spoken very sternly to the driver of the bus (which of course I had). I explained that it had been a 'Mr Johnson', a supply teacher, who had only been with us a few weeks, and that he was very sorry for his unacceptable road manners. I went on to reassure her that he would never again repeat this sort of behaviour in one of our school buses for fear of finding himself an ex-supply teacher.

Having told my story, I enquired as to whether the fact that 'Mr Johnson' had been so severely reprimanded was sufficient indication of how seriously I took her concerns.

'Of course!' she replied, adding that she was grateful for my call and the swiftness with which I had dealt with the problem. She ended the conversation by saying she was more than happy to leave the matter of disciplinary action in my obviously capable hands.

Even now I cannot pass a similar make of minibus without feeling a twinge of conscience. I offer my confession for your wise judgement . . .

A Repentant Head Teacher

Too Hot To Handle

Dear Father Mayo,

I beg your forgiveness. Over twenty years ago, in the mid-1980s when I was fifteen years old, I tried to earn a bit of extra pocket money by waitressing a couple of nights a week at a local restaurant.

This small family-run establishment was well known, and the food was so good that it was even frequented by some VIPs and a celebrity cook – who still lives in the area. The set-up was small scale, with the chef and one assistant working in the kitchen, his formidable wife running the restaurant, and every now and again an extra, very inexperienced waitress – me.

Now, this restaurant was famous for one particular dish, an incredible fish soup, served with secret ingredients, a delicious mayonnaise and croutons. I had been given a little to try on one occasion, and I can confirm it was indeed a very fine soup. It was brought to the table in a huge terrine, with a ladle balanced in the dish for the waitress to serve it to the individual diners at the table.

One night, when a table ordered the special dish, I was called by the chef to collect it from the kitchen. The delicious aroma of the legendary creation attacked my nostrils and caused my mouth to start watering. Between the kitchen area and the restaurant was a small length of corridor, a kind of no-man's-land, not visible from either end. The temptation was too great. I gingerly balanced the heavy soup terrine in one hand, lifted the ladle with the other and poured the fish soup straight into my mouth.

What I hadn't considered, of course, was the fact that the soup, fresh from the hot plate, would be scalding.

There I was in the corridor, unable to scream or make any noise at all, for fear of making my transgression known. The boiling liquid began peeling the skin away from the roof of my mouth and I was in agony. Terrified the chef's wife would catch me, I did the only thing I could – I spat the soup back into the terrine, along with the bits of skin from the roof of my mouth.

A few seconds passed as I tried to compose myself and work out what to do next, then I heard footsteps approaching from the kitchen. There was simply no other option. I straightened my posture, held my head high and walked confidently out into the restaurant where I served the soup to the poor, unsuspecting diners, who had no idea there was a little extra ingredient amongst the mussels and monkfish.

I ask for forgiveness for my dreadful deed. I learned my lesson and never did it again!

Jane

The French Mis-connection

Dear Father Simon,

I am seeking your forgiveness for two acts that were committed more than ten years ago, but over which I still lose sleep today. These acts took place in 1998 while I was on a twelve-month assignment in the South of France for a well-known IT company. The team was international and comprised a fascinating blend of languages and cultures; and this combined with the stresses and strains of a weekly commute to France meant that day-to-day life was a highly charged affair. We all worked together, we all lived in the same hotel and we all socialized with one another – so if someone irritated you, even slightly, this could quickly drive you to breaking point.

One such person, whom we will call Richie, was the most irritating of all. He would talk incessantly and liked to do so while standing just a few inches away from your face. It was hard enough with him climbing into your personal space, but the main problem was that he would often receive calls on his mobile from friends in the UK, and then force the phone on to you so you could speak to them, whether you knew them or not. Pushing your hands into your pockets did nothing to deter him and he'd do his best to press the earpiece to the side of your head. Being in the presence of Richie night and day drove me to the point of madness and I did everything I could to avoid him, which, given our circumstances, was near on impossible.

Our offices were in a converted factory and had no air-conditioning to protect us from the crippling heat. Apart from avoiding acute dehydration, our other main problem was an infestation of tiny black fruit flies. They seemed to get into everything and made you feel itchy and uncomfortable, and nothing whatsoever could be done to move them on. Life became a constant cycle of sweating in the heat, dodging Richie and splatting tiny black flies, day after day after day.

Is it any wonder I cracked?

So, I devised a plan, of which I am both proud and ashamed.

The company I worked for operated an 'empty your own bin' policy and, as we didn't have the luxury of office cleaners, I decided to use this to my advantage. One Friday evening when the office was empty, I got hold of an empty waste-paper bin. Taking a couple of bananas, I squashed them up, skins and all, and threw them in. I then pushed the bin out of sight and as far under Richie's desk as I could before leaving for the weekend.

On returning to work after a scorching weekend it was evident that the volume of black flies had considerably diminished. Wonder where they went?

I then set about fixing my other problem, Richie's mobile. I waited for my opportunity and as soon as he left his phone unguarded, I grabbed it and diverted all his incoming calls to a London-based ticket office for a well-known live music venue. I dread to think what Richie's phone bill would have been as his calls bounced around from the UK to France and back again.

By Tuesday evening my fly trap must have matured to the point that most of the flies had decided to live there, and I also noticed that Richie seemed to have developed an incessant itching around his leg regions. It was clear from his face that all was not well – his preoccupation with his rash left him little time to annoy us, and now we would see him pacing around, alone and itchy and in need of *la pharmacie*.

Things were brought to a head on Wednesday afternoon. During a break by the coffee machine I was joined by an ashen-faced Richie, who explained in distressed tones that he had been having 'terrible problems' with his legs and why the hell wouldn't his GP call him back as he'd requested.

Guilt drove me to end my plan and I removed the bin that evening. Being fully populated, my banana bucket had become the stuff of nightmares, and my vision of the sheer volume of flies still haunts me today. The thought of Richie sat at his desk alternating between scratching his legs and checking his phone for a missed call from his bewildered doctor only increased my sense of guilt.

Needless to say, he eventually made a full recovery, although he did end up being labelled as 'Itchy Richie', which I understand may have caused a little relationship problem or two.

And so ends my confession. Your forgiveness would be gratefully received. I'm sorry, Richie.

Yours, 'Guilty' of Yorkshire

The Great Molar Mix-up

Father Simon and the gathered Collective,

I seek forgiveness for a misdemeanour that happened many years ago when I had just left school.

I was thrilled at getting my first job as a dental technician at a very upmarket surgery in my local town. The people were friendly and I very much enjoyed working there. There was only one drawback. The boss. He was a rather uptight and rude man who thought himself better than any of the other dentists in town, and probably in the county. None of the dental nurses liked working with him, and they all dreaded publication of the monthly rota that would see them paired with him at some point in the next four weeks.

My main job at this time was to take impressions of patients' mouths to fit them for false teeth, dental braces and mouth guards. This was an expensive and laborious process both for the patient and the technician, as it meant weeks of fitting, refitting and adjusting to get the final product just right.

The first stage of the process was the creation of a wax mould of the patient's teeth, which was then tested for fit at the next appointment. It was then recast and retested, again and again. The waxworks were carefully labelled several times in different places so they would not get mixed up. Once the mould was just right, it was sent away to be turned into the final thing. It was a long process that could take up to three months.

One day I was summoned into the surgery for a 'chat' with the horrible dentist. Knees knocking, I entered, wondering why he wanted me. After a brief dressing-down about my appearance and the clothes I wore (it was the 1980s), I was given notice for 'not being right' for their image. I was shocked, and gutted as I really enjoyed my job. He told me to leave on Friday so I had only three days left.

This is when my plan for revenge began to develop. On my last day, I had several patients coming in for a final fitting. I made sure everything was spot on, then labelled the pieces and took them to the lab. In the lab, I set about swapping all the names around. The impression for an elderly lady's new false teeth was swapped with a teenage rugby player's mouth guard, the rugby player ended up with an eight-year-old's new brace, who in turn ended up with the cast for a middle-aged solicitor's new dentures, and so on. I placed the wrongly marked casts into the bags and sent them away for making. All in all I created chaos for twelve patients.

I did stay in touch with one or two friends from the clinic and so I learned of the outcome of my handiwork, and I can tell you it caused uproar, not only damaging the reputation of the practice in the community (after all, the twelve unlucky victims of my work had already been waiting for three months) but also costing it a large amount of money as they repeated twelve moulding and casting processes, a cost that would have run into the thousands even then.

Father Simon, I seek forgiveness, not from the horrible dentist, but from the patients, who were looking forward to having teeth again and had to start the long laborious process of fitting from scratch. I also seek forgiveness from the poor dental nurses, who no doubt were on the sharp end of this man's wrath.

Please forgive me, Simon. I know it was wrong of me and I still think about the incident many years later.

Jane

The Doctor Will See You Now

Dear Father Simon and the Confessional Collective,

I would like my identity to remain secret because these days I am a respectable consultant neurosurgeon, and I would not like to shake the confidence of the patients who place their trust in me. However, since my training days as a student in a reputable teaching hospital, I have carried with me a burden of guilt after an indiscretion born of youthful exuberance and fuelled, it shames me to say, Simon, by a certain quantity of alcohol.

I had been on call with my medical team for a long weekend, which in the 1970s was typically Friday morning until Monday evening. It had been a weekend with the usual mix of drunks who had fallen or fought, or both, peppered with a sprinkling of young and elderly with various conditions. Weekends on call were hectic and stressful, and it was customary on completion of such a prolonged duty stint to let your hair down on the Monday night.

The qualified junior medical staff had to keep one eye on the need to show up in reasonable condition for work as usual on Tuesday morning. However, for the unqualified medical student, the junior doctors would offer to turn a blind eye to a late arrival or even failure to show the following day, taking the stance that 'you are only young once'.

On the occasion in question, I took full advantage of my immediate bosses' generosity. I partied into the night and indeed through the night, staggering home bleary-eyed, not thinking entirely straight, the following morning. I summoned all my concentration to make my way to the doctors' residence, and followed the most direct route, *which involved a shortcut through the A&E department.*

It was in the course of this shortcut that I transgressed. You see, the continual flow of pints was by now having an acute and entirely predictable effect on my bladder. The discomfort was by this time excruciating, and the need to remedy this was so pressing that waiting until reaching the doctors' residence was just not an option.

In fact, so urgent was the need that even identifying a toilet in A&E was not an option either. I pushed open the nearest door and, on registering that the room beyond was in darkness, I stepped inside, the door swinging shut behind, obliterating all light. I felt my way along the wall, thinking that any plumbing would have to do, even if it was only a sink. But the need was now overwhelming, and on detecting a tall metal pedal bin with my fumbling hands, I decided this would have to do. There was soon a loud drumming sound as my bladder emptied into the bin.

My relief was audible, but suddenly, much to my confusion, the room was filled with skull-splitting light. As I tried to make sense of what was going on, I looked over my shoulder. And there, as my eyes adjusted to the blaze of light, I saw the professor of ophthalmology conducting an eye examination on an elderly lady. You see, I had mistakenly, drunkenly, made my way into an examination room.

So, Father Simon and Collective, I ask for forgiveness, not for upsetting the professor, whom I'd never been overly keen on anyway, and who subsequently threatened at the top of his voice to terminate my embryonic medical career. And I'm not sure that the elderly lady really was too badly affected, as her sight can hardly have been 20/20, and she probably struggled to make sense of what she had heard.

No, I ask for forgiveness because, having recently allowed a teenage party to take place in my own house, I now understand how unpleasant it is to find 'effluvia' in the bin, and realize that an unfortunate hospital domestic must have received a similarly unpleasant shock in 1978.

Yours repentantly, Brain Surgeon

The Great Denture Duplicity

Dear Father Mayo and Assembled Collective,

In the 1960s I was a student nurse doing my training in a large city hospital. On the day in question I was gaining experience on an elderly female ward, and one of the patients had died. I shall call her Mrs A. This ward, by the way, was of the 'nightingale' type, very long with the patients' beds lining the walls on two sides, each separated by a small locker.

The staff nurse decided it was time I learned the rudiments of 'last offices': nursing terminology for laying out the deceased. So together, behind closed curtains, we set about making Mrs A look as peaceful and pleasant as possible for when her relatives came to say their goodbyes. This involved washing Mrs A, brushing her hair, fitting her dentures and generally a lot of TLC, as you would expect under such circumstances.

Later that day, long after Mrs A had been dispatched to the hospital mortuary, I noticed that the lady in the bed next to her appeared very upset. I shall call her Mrs B. I went over with the intention of reassuring her and comforting her over the demise of Mrs A, but soon realized this wasn't the reason for her distress. No, she was upset because she couldn't get her dentures to fit. They appeared to be far too big.

After trying to help her, without success, the truth began to dawn on me. Mrs B's dentures were now resting safely in Mrs A in the mortuary. I knew I was to blame because I had not checked they were the correct ones before fitting them, and being smaller they had gone in reasonably well. I had to think quickly. Luckily for me it was Sister's day off, and as soon as staff nurse went for her 15-minute break, I took my opportunity.

Taking the dentures from a somewhat confused and now surprised Mrs B (who was unable to object effectively as she had no teeth), I said I'd take them to the hospital workshop to sort them out, then sprinted out of the ward, down two flights of stairs, across two floors, across the hospital car park and over to the far corner of the grounds to the mortuary. After much pleading and begging to the mortuary attendant, I was finally, grudgingly, allowed in, and between us we managed to remove Mrs B's dentures from the now chilled Mrs A, and replace them with her own. Not easy.

With Mrs B's dentures in my pocket, I sprinted back to the ward, hot and bothered but thankfully not missed. I gave the teeth a quick scrub behind the nurses' station, then made my way back to Mrs B's bedside, my best nurse's smile on my face.

Thankfully Mrs B's visitors were just arriving, and no explanation was asked for or given. As she happily slid her shiny dentures into her mouth, I couldn't help but feel a shiver go down my spine, knowing where they had been just minutes before.

The mortuary attendant never spilled the beans and I got away with my horrible mistake. Can I be forgiven, please? If it helps my case, I went on to qualify as a nurse and then eventually as a sister, which I remained for thirty-seven years.

Ann

Pranks

Oh, don't we love a prankster? Well, the answer is no, we don't. The brothers and sisters of the Confessional Collective find jokers and tricksters to be A COMPLETE PAIN IN THE NECK. And they never get forgiven either, even when they are actually quite funny. The custard pie last raised a laugh in 1934 and the whoopee cushion in 1870. So be warned, all you hilarious funsters, that we HAVE HAD ENOUGH OF YOUR STUPIDITY, THANK YOU VERY MUCH. You can stop now.

Off Your Trolley

Hi Simon and the Collective,

I wish to fall before the divine Collective and beg forgiveness for something that happened a few years ago.

First, I would like to dispel the myth that men hate shopping. We don't. What we object to is the constant checking and rechecking and trying on the same thing yet again just to be sure it's OK, then taking it back a week later because someone has changed their mind.

The weekly supermarket shop, while not subject to these particular tortures, is nevertheless not the most exciting thing and within a short time I would always get bored.

One day, I bumped into a male friend who was also out shopping with his wife, and we got talking. It turned out that due to job changes they would be shopping on the same day as us on a regular basis. Mischievous plans started to form in our minds within seconds of this news, and we both knew it.

Over the next few weeks it started quite jovially really. You know, the usual thing of slipping something into the other person's trolley and hoping they only notice after they have paid the bill. I mean, if you don't notice six pairs of rubber gloves or fifty beef burgers at the checkout, you are clearly not paying attention.

But after a while this became a little mundane, so a new game was born, a kind of 'catching' game. We agreed to get to a specific point down two parallel aisles and then one of us would throw an item over the top of the shelves and the other would try to catch it. It was always light things like dishcloths or crisp packets, which were easy. On one particular day I was expecting the usual thing to come over the shelves, but instead a large bag of frozen peas appeared, which I didn't catch. The bag hit the edge of the trolley, split open and peas scattered in all directions. Feeling bad, I tried to clear up as many as I could while listening to much laughter coming from the aisle next door. I apologized to the frowning shop worker who had joined me to help clear up, telling him the bag had burst when I picked it up. He seemed to believe me.

After this, the game wasn't played again. I didn't really want to spend the afternoon clearing up the mess on the floor of my local supermarket.

Then, a few weeks later, this time both of us tackling the weekly shop alone, I bumped into the same friend. We had a good old laugh about the pea incident and then we went about our business. A little later, I was minding my own business nearing the end of the mammoth shop, when I heard the word 'Incoming!' Not really sure who this was meant for, I looked up, only to see a large family-sized frozen chicken flying through the air towards me. I naturally moved out of the way and watched this piece of hard, iced poultry smash into my trolley and destroy a number of items inside. I stood there speechless, watching a puddle of milk, fruit juice and broken eggs gradually spread out on the floor beneath, causing a huge, unpleasant and expanding mess. I decided that abandoning the trolley and leaving the store quickly was the best course of action. My retaliatory litre bottle of salad cream was, I realize, unhelpful.

I seek forgiveness, not for the incident itself but for leaving a mess that some poor store worker would have had to clear up. Perhaps the same man as before. I also seek forgiveness for the items in the trolley, which probably had to be thrown away.

Yours on grovelling knees, Paul

Chew'll Never Walk Alone

Dear Father Simon,

I feel I must confess to a small incident that happened about five or six years ago. My husband is a Liverpool football fan and it had been a long-held dream to watch his team play at their famous home ground, Anfield. While not as enthusiastic as him, I went along to give 'wifely moral support' – and to avoid having to do ironing and so forth. We got into the ground and the game started, and my husband was teary-eyed as they sang 'You'll Never Walk Alone'.

I had taken along bagfuls of sweets and goodies to get me through the game. Well, I got a bit bored and couldn't see much, especially as the man in front of me was on the large side. All through the game he kept on standing up and sitting down, standing up and sitting down, as they do. It was particularly painful to watch when he sat down, as he revealed about three inches of backside cleavage. Anyway, after a while, I fancied a sweet, but first I had to get rid of the bright green gum I had been steadily chewing. I took the gum from my mouth, thinking I would put it in the sweet wrapper.

However, as I took it out of my mouth, I had a sudden involuntary movement, and the chewing gum flicked down the back of the large man's backside area. I could see it perched, precariously, between his belt and the offending cleavage. I stared at it for a few seconds, wondering if I should tell him, when the team scored. Up he jumped and, as he did so, I saw the gum disappear down into the depths of his pants region. I spent the rest of the game wondering if

I should tap him on the shoulder and admit what I had done. In the end I did the right thing – I said nothing.

I confessed to my husband on the way home, who thought the incident a brilliant ending to a good day watching his team. I, however, should really seek forgiveness from the rather large football fan who, when he got home, had no doubt to get a wife or perhaps mother or indeed friend to extract the gum from his nether regions. Worse still, he may have worried as to why he was excreting green chewy stuff.

So, Father Simon and the team, I ask your forgiveness because it was a total accident, and I haven't been to the football since as I just don't trust myself.

'Mrs B'

Act Your Beige

Simon,

My tale begins a couple of years ago, when my daughter rang me at work. She wasn't her usual bubbly self. In fact, Simon, she was in floods of tears and I could barely work out what she was saying as she blubbered down the phone. After a while she calmed down and explained what had been upsetting her. She had bought a pair of shoes for her 18-month-old daughter, but one sole was defective and had fallen off. When she returned to the shop, complete with the receipt and the shoebox, ready for a friendly figure to apologize and rectify the situation, she was surprised instead to find a senior staff member accusing her young daughter of causing the damage. Doing her best to maintain composure, my daughter explained that the child had only just started to walk and this was just not possible. But no, he was not prepared to do anything about it, no exchange, no refund, no repair – and rudely told her to go away.

On hearing this, I was not happy, to say the least. I told her not to worry and that I would sort it out immediately. As it happened, I was suited and booted from a meeting I had just attended. So I told my work colleagues I had to pop out and, minutes later, after a short drive, I pulled up right in front of the large shoe shop in my flashy sports car and went in, Filofax and mobile in hand, looking like a real mover and shaker. I started to look around the shop and it was then that I was approached by, to quote my daughter's words, the 'horrible man who bullied young mums', whom I immediately recognized from her description of him.

Thinking on my feet – appropriately enough – I told him I was the boss of a travelling theatre company (I don't know where that came from!) and needed to buy as many beige shoes, in as many sizes, as he could let me have for a play we were putting on that very evening. Again, why I chose the colour beige, I don't know. Well, Simon, his eyes lit up and so began the full smarm offensive. Ignoring every other customer in the shop, he ordered all of his staff to pull out all the beige shoes they could find. Those poor ladies were soon running up and down the stairs and darting up ladders getting out all the beige stock they could lay their hands on, while he gave them their orders, all the time beaming at me and calling me 'Madam'.

The pile got bigger and bigger until there were hundreds of pairs, causing me to get a bit nervous – but I let it carry on. He then crept over to me and said that was his entire stock 'in beige'. I said, 'Fantastic, I will be sure to mention your shop in our theatre programme.' I calmly asked for the bill, and he then ordered a poor soul to start putting every single pair through the till. When she had finished this marathon, he proudly presented me with the three-foot bill. Such was his pleasure at such a huge sale for a passing VIP that he'd even managed to find a small silver tray to present my bill on. Taking this travelling theatrical motif to the next level, I opened my wallet, acted shocked to the best of my ability and told him, 'Oh, I am sorry, I must have left my credit card outside in the car!'

However, I asked him to carry on and bag them all up for me as quickly as he could, as I needed to get my new beige footwear wardrobe to rehearsals as soon as possible.

So I left the shop, got into my car and, of course, never went back. At the time I felt so good, as I am sure parents will understand. But I have always felt ashamed of doing this and I would just like to say sorry, not to the manager, but to the poor ladies who worked for him, as I am sure they had to put all of them back and suffer his wrath.

Sue

PS My daughter was delighted with me!

Dental Duplicity

Dear Father Simon and the Confessional Collective,

As a respectable dentist with my own practice in a nice market town, I obviously need to be very careful about the identities of those involved in this tale. So for purposes of this story you can call me Dr Bob; all other names are changed to protect, well, me mainly!

The story goes back at least twenty years, when I was a young associate working in a practice in another market town, not quite as nice as the one I'm in now, but still quite respectable. You were on the radio in the mornings, doing similar old tosh to entertain the country on their way to work as you do now while they're coming home.

My tale involves cartons of a very popular blackcurrant drink. My nurse at the time was a lovely girl called Gina and she loved that particular brand. She probably got through two or three cartons a day (which, as a dentist, I didn't feel had a totally positive effect on her teeth).

Now, presumably to sell more cartons of their product, the company decided to run a promotion. The premise was that Larry the Lime had invaded a few cartons. If your blackcurrant drink tasted of lime, you could win up to £10,000, which was a lot of money in Thatcher's Britain – and frankly still is. Gina and I had always enjoyed the odd joke with each other, and I came up with a cunning master plan. One night, I took home one of her empty cartons and set to work. I mixed up some lime cordial and carefully refilled the carton, using a (clean) syringe from work. The only problem was I couldn't reseal the little hole which you poke the straw through. So, I would need to engineer a switch very carefully.

The next day I came to work – listening to my favourite DJ on Radio 1's breakfast show on the way in, obviously – and surreptitiously hid the carton, with straw in place, in the cupboard behind my surgery chair. The day was warm, we didn't have air-conditioning and the fixing of the local population's teeth was thirsty work, so my hopes were high that Gina would soon be requiring a drink. But nothing happened at first.

At about eleven o'clock, Mrs Jones came in for an extraction. I administered the local anaesthetic and sat back while it worked. Gina went into reception and, to my delight, came back with an unopened carton of her favourite drink.

Timing was now everything. I desperately looked round for something we didn't have. As soon as Gina pushed in the straw, I struck. 'Oh, Gina,' I said, 'I'm on my last pair of gloves, could you just pop and get another box?'

The look on her face said 'Won't it wait till we've finished, I was just about to have a drink . . .' but like the dutiful nurse she was, she went to the cupboard to fetch a new box. This gave me just long enough to switch her carton with the one I'd prepared earlier. She returned with the gloves, sat down, passed me the probe so I could check the patient was numb, then passed me the forceps to remove the manky molar. I set to work.

Gina moved her chair back to the worktop, picked up her carton and took a slurp. Being a professional, I carried on with my task, even though I could see Gina's face register first surprise at the unexpected taste of her drink, then realization. She took another sip, and a smile spread from ear to ear. A sort of 'I've just won 10,000 pounds' smile.

I managed to complete the task, removing the molar cleanly and painlessly, although I think the patient might have noticed a slight shaking as I was trying my hardest not to laugh out loud. Gina was, in her head, already dancing round the surgery as she spent her new fortune.

The patient left. Gina, having reread the Larry the Lime promotion details on the outside, was now hacking into the carton with a scalpel to see what prize she had won. The vigour of her knife work reminded me of the shower scene in *Psycho* . . . Imagine her surprise when she found there was nothing on the inside telling her she had won £10,000. There was nothing telling her she had won any of the other lovely prizes. In fact, there was nothing at all.

I never confessed to Gina. After all, I'd seen her in action with a scalpel.

So, primarily, I suppose, I'm seeking forgiveness from Gina, who never understood why £10,000 wasn't hers and I never had the bottle to tell her. Also, I think I owe the manufacturer of the beverage an apology, especially the customer service operative who fielded Gina's irate calls. The shareholders of the company should also be mentioned in dispatches – they must have suffered decreased dividends as Gina never bought another carton of the drink. Finally, I feel I should say sorry to Mrs Jones, the lady who was having the extraction. She didn't suffer, but she must have left thinking her dentist had a mild case of the DTs. In mitigation, I'm sure Gina's teeth will forgive me. She switched to much more tooth-friendly bottled water after the disappointment of not winning ten grand. And saving people's teeth is my job.

Yours in humble remorse, Dr Bob

Pond Life

Dear Father, Mother and Children,

My story goes back to the 1970s when I was a medical student, sharing a large house with five other med students, doing the usual stuff.

All was well at the time except for one thing . . . the landlord. He lived in the adjacent house, and he was like Rigsby in *Rising Damp* but without the charm. He'd bang on the walls if the music was too loud or if we were larking around, and he was always letting himself into the house without warning. We never said anything to upset him in case he sent us packing.

One night we were all sitting around having a drink and moaning about Rigsby and wondering how we could get our revenge. At the time he was digging a hole in his garden for a fish pond. We thought about filling it back in halfway every night so the job would take for ever, but then one of the guys looked over at an item that had pride of place in the house and said, 'Why not bury Lord Lucan in the plot for Rigsby to discover?' Lord Lucan, I should explain here, was the name we gave to our model skeleton.

We all agreed it was a great idea, so in the dead of night we crept next door, giggling like a bunch of schoolgirls, placed the skeleton in the hole, gave him a pair of sunglasses as a finishing touch and covered him over with soil, returning to the house for a few more drinks, trying not to laugh too loudly.

Next morning we awoke to Rigsby's bloodcurdling screams. 'CALL THE POLICE! CALL THE POLICE! HELP! HELP!' His wife was in a similar state of hysteria. We gathered at our window to watch the reaction to our revenge, but we were not expecting what happened next. After a few minutes, a couple of police officers turned up, and we began to worry. When a forensic team turned up, we all legged it out of the house, because now we knew we could be in serious trouble.

We hid out of sight behind a wall in the front garden, waiting for it all to end. After a while, we heard raised voices as the police and forensic teams – who had now discovered that a bunch of medical students were responsible for this – made their way out of his house. Rigsby was subjected to a doorstep dressing-down for wasting their time, and his intelligence was further called into question by his not having realized that the sunglasses kind of suggested it was nothing more than a prank. Shamefaced, he shuffled back into his house, and nothing was ever said to us about the incident. One good thing to come out of it was that he never bothered us much after that. He never completed his pond either.

Father, I would like to ask for forgiveness, not from Rigsby, who got the shock he deserved, but from the police for the time we wasted.

'Dr Dunalot'

The Alarming Affliction

Dear Father Simon and the Confessional Team,

My tale stretches back to 1983 when I was a man of twenty-two living in the south of England following a transfer with work from my home town in Scotland. I had rented a pleasant flat near the station but soon realized that before the end of each month I was always penniless and drifting into an ever-increasing overdraft. Action was urgently required. I decided to rent out the two spare rooms in the flat to lodgers. The first were a couple of 'likely lads' I had recently met and both turned out to be great flatmates. They shared a room, which left another to rent out.

The next applicant was a young guy, also from Scotland, called David. On the face of it he seemed OK, so he got the room, but as time went on he turned into the flatmate from hell. He always had something to complain about, whether it was untidiness, three days' worth of dishes in the sink or food stolen from the fridge. David, who worked in IT, was also a bit of a geek. He was, frankly, boring. He never chilled out with us at the local hostelry, never joined in the fun at the many parties we held. Instead he chose to be rude, complaining and awkward at all times.

Another point to note is that David's casual wardrobe was unvarying. He always wore the same green checked shirt and a pair of jeans with great big turn-ups. (Told you he was a geek!) And thus was my plan hatched . . .

Every Saturday, David would take the train into town and shop for geeky things to add to his home IT set-up. On one particularly hot Saturday in July, he returned to the flat in a distressed state and revealed that he had been apprehended in a computer store for suspected shoplifting. After much questioning by security staff and the police, he was finally released from the store manager's office. We displayed our concern over this with sympathetic tones all round, and the incident was soon forgotten.

On the following Saturday, however, we had a repeat performance. David arrived back at the flat even more distressed at having been apprehended once again, this time in a well-known electrical store. It began to happen every time David went into not only electrical stores but also clothing shops or indeed anywhere there was an electronic tag detector to prevent shoplifting.

The ultimate Saturday incident was when David, now almost at the point of a breakdown and totally paranoid about shops, came back to tell us he had been strip-searched at the local police station after yet another 'shoplifting' incident. As on all previous occasions, they had found no stolen goods on or around his person.

David finally decided that his future in England was gloomy and moved back to Scotland for sanctuary, leaving behind a glittering career in IT. My confession then, albeit almost thirty years late, comes in the form of my association with a manager at a well-known department store. Let's call her Mandy.

Having learned of my frustration with David, Mandy agreed to lend me a 'fix it' piece of equipment, in the form of one of the little chips contained in the security tags from her store. This had been carefully inserted in a turn-up of David's infamous jeans. The result, of course, being that each time he left a store with a tag detector, it would activate the alarm and he would be swarmed by security staff, and eventually the police.

David's final eight months in the south must have been a nightmare and I never did keep in touch to find out what he ended up doing. Presumably he took his jeans back to Scotland and I can only assume he had the same problems there too.

So, Father Simon, I look now for forgiveness so that I can finally sleep peacefully at night.

Regards, Paul

Island Hopping

Dear Simon and Team,

I would like to confess to a sin committed many years ago: 1994, in fact. I know this is a long time ago but the fallout and entanglements that resulted have only now got to a stage where I can even think of doing this. I have also opted for the pseudonym of Xavier. If one is to use a pseudonym, it might as well be a cool one.

I am a biologist and, when I was twenty-two, I was working on an island in the Indian Ocean with a female biologist. I cannot be more precise about this – the conservation biology world is indeed a small one. We were working alone there, restoring populations of endangered plants, reptiles and birds. I hope the worthiness of this task will help my cause in your eyes. The female biologist – let's call her Carmen (well, she might as well have a cool name too) – was, and still is, gorgeous. Having spent a couple of months together, we became very close. However, much to my dismay, and shyness, nothing ever happened between us. Then I had a boating accident and injured my arm, requiring a short stay in the hospital on the mainland. It was agreed that Carmen would return to the island on her own while my injuries were dealt with, and then return in the boat in a few days' time to pick me up.

I could also see I was beginning to add another emotion into the mix at this stage – sympathy, on her part.

Things, however, did not go to plan. I was released early from hospital and thought I would surprise her by hitching a lift back from a friendly fisherman. I also brought her some flowers, but alas I left them on the boat. Having made it back to the island safe and sound, albeit empty-handed, I went to our shared accommodation. I made myself a cup of tea and went into the living area to drink it. On my way, I heard Carmen whistling as she walked down the path to the house.

A moment of madness took over and I hid in a cupboard. The romantic gesture of surprising her became a childish one of being given the opportunity to go 'boo!' Through the gaps in the cupboard door I could see her inspecting the freshly made tea with some puzzlement. Then she shrugged and went into the kitchen. I slipped out of the cupboard, drank the tea and slipped back in again. I was beside myself with mirth and had to bite my lip to stop myself from laughing out loud. She came back into the room and saw the cup was empty. Again she had a puzzled look on her face, this time tinged with confusion, even a touch of fear. She put down the sandwich she had made, took the cup and went back to the kitchen. I couldn't help myself. I once more slipped out of my hiding place, took a bite out of her sandwich and hid again.

She came back with a cup of tea to wash down her sandwich, only to see it had been bitten into. She began to look a little scared. I, however, had gone beyond the point of no return. It was no longer funny, but if I stepped out and said anything, it would have ruined any potential for future romance with this lovely lady. Indeed, she would only have been angry with me for a very long time. To make matters even worse, the room was getting a bit draughty, and on another of her absences I slipped out to close a window and snatch my jacket from the back of a chair, adding to her confusion and now very real fear.

I hid quietly, and the evening wore on with a very frightened Carmen jumping at every noise and retiring early to her room. I slept in the cupboard. In the morning I woke up, cramped and sore, and slipped out and went to the kitchen. Enough was enough and I was going to confess. Carmen awoke a few minutes later and came into the kitchen to find me there. She asked how I had got back to the island.

Despite my best intentions, I lied and told her I had been dropped off by a friendly fisherman about ten minutes ago. She promptly threw her arms around me in relief that I was back and told me that she thought she was losing her mind. The story does not end here, Simon and team, oh no. I could not confess even then, and over the next few years never really got the opportunity or found the courage to as we embarked on a relationship that lasted many years.

I now humbly ask for your forgiveness for what must have been very frightening for a lady alone on an island in the Indian Ocean.

Yours sincerely, 'Xavier'

A *Classic* Error

Dear Simon,

I want to confess to a wanton act of cultural vandalism that has preyed on my mind for many years.

In the late 1970s I was a young and irresponsible student at university doing engineering. I admit that, apart from my studies, my main objective was having a good time, and I had little interest in the finer things in life.

One particularly hot summer's evening, I left the Students' Union bar to pick up something from my room on the campus. Although the night was still young, I had already spent a considerable amount of my student grant in the bar. On my way back to the bar from my room, I happened to pass by the main hall of the university, and I noticed there was something going on. Curious, I went over to get a better look. The windows were open, and I was able to see hundreds of smartly dressed people listening to a large orchestra surrounded by lots of equipment. I listened intently as the orchestra played on and finally reached a crescendo of noise. This I found out later is called a first movement.

After a few moments the orchestra started playing again, this time slowly and very quietly. This I later found out is called a slow movement. However, to me it was boring and nowhere near as exciting as the first bit.

For reasons that shall forever remain a mystery, I suddenly remembered Eric Morecambe of Morecambe and Wise and his famous catchphrase, 'What do you think of it so far?'

The inevitable response sprang to mind and I found myself shouting 'RUBBISH!' at the top of my voice during a particularly quiet part of the music. I have been blessed with a voice that could double as a foghorn, and most of the faces in the packed hall turned towards the open windows in the direction the noise had come from. No one looked at all pleased so I thought it best to leave the scene at high speed.

I returned to the bar where the jukebox was blasting out some livelier, more student-friendly tunes, and thought nothing more of it until the next day, when lots of people were talking about the events of the previous night.

Apparently, after long preparation and planning, one of the world's top orchestras had come to play at the university, but their concert had been ruined by heckling from an unknown bystander. As if this wasn't bad enough, the concert was being broadcast live to the nation on BBC Radio 3. On urgent reflection, I decided the consequences of revealing myself as the mystery heckler might be severe, so until this day my identity has remained a secret.

Simon, I crave forgiveness for spoiling the enjoyment of those fine people and ruining an event that had been months in preparation. I apologize to the orchestra and those in the BBC involved in broadcasting the concert, and lastly I apologize to those listening at home that night, who must have been puzzled, if not disturbed, to hear someone shouting 'RUBBISH!' in the middle of a beautifully moving piece of music. These days I quite like classical music, so please release me from my guilty torment.

Michael

A Bolt from the Loo

Dear Simon and the Collective,

A few years ago, I spent my spare time as a historical re-enactor. For the uninitiated, let me explain that we are the people you find in castles or muddy fields dressed as people from the past and posturing with our shiny swords. Now, I should first beg forgiveness for some minor transgressions: a coconut left in a display of medieval English fruit, a small stuffed toy rabbit used in anger during the Battle of Hastings, that kind of thing.

One Friday in the early 1990s, we were due to go and occupy a castle on the coast, and there was the usual manic preparation involved in forcing a small army and all its equipment into a van. Part of my task involved me going round to my friend Nige's house to pick up his stuff, as he was at work. I should point out here that the weapons we use are quite safe; all the edged ones are blunted, all the blunt weapons are . . . well, they are safe too. All the bows are 'low poundage', meaning they are weaker than the real ones, and our arrows and bolts are rubber-tipped. But we do have display weapons that are more powerful, and use real metal-tipped arrows and bolts to show people – let's just say it's educational.

So, arriving at Nige's flat, imagine my glee when I saw a bright shiny new crossbow he had not mentioned. Now, there is history in that flat on the matter of crossbows, because it had a really long corridor from the front door to the loo at the far end, long enough to use as a shooting gallery, and we had in the past safely tested all manner of weapons against either the loo door or a pile of telephone directories balanced on the WC. At once, I realized two things: a) I was there on my own, and b) the crossbow had not yet been used.

My hands clasped it with sheer lust and I started to crank it up, ready for the shot. It was quite powerful – it needed a special crank to wind it – so I wisely piled two phonebooks on the loo behind the old dartboard that we used as a target. I aimed and shot. There was a thwack as the bolt sailed through the directories and was brought up sharply by the cistern behind it. I was both spooked and enraptured, and quickly assessed the damage: a slightly bent tip to the bolt (easily straightened), a hole in the dartboard (quickly filled), and a barely seen hairline crack in the cistern that had obviously been there before and was therefore nothing to do with me. I set up for a second shot, but realizing the time, replaced the holed directories at the bottom of the pile, grabbed what I needed to and left the crossbow exactly where I had found it, albeit now ready to shoot.

We had a nice trip down to the coast. We got to the site, and it was then that I realized Nige hadn't joined us.

'Oh, he had to stay behind, his toilet has exploded,' said somebody matter-of-factly.

I gulped.

'Silly fool was practising with that new crossbow he ordered,' said somebody else. 'He shot the loo and it exploded.'

'Oh really?' I said.

'Yep. He is trying to get a plumber, or a new loo from somewhere, so he may not be with us this weekend.'

It turned out that when Nige had gone home, he had also looked at the crossbow, had the same thought as me and had cranked it up hard. After all, it had just arrived from the maker and they would never send it cranked up through the post! How powerful his shot from the double-cranked crossbow would have been is probably best not thought about. The bolt flew straight through the dartboard (which it destroyed), through two telephone directories (the thick ones, which it destroyed), through the cistern (which could take no more and shattered), the back of the cistern (destroyed), a pipe (holed, bent, useless), through the wall and into the back garden where it scared a cat and sank into the lawn.

I would like to appeal to the Collective and beg forgiveness. From Nige, who had to spend the weekend fitting a toilet; from his landlord, who had a leaky loo to deal with; from the cat, who developed a nervous fear of the garden, and from the maker of the crossbow who had to fend off irate phone calls from Nige about sending wound-up crossbows through the post. But most of all, I would like to beg the forgiveness of the crossbow, which was never the same and only ever managed two decent shots in its short existence before it broke a couple of weeks later . . .

Dave

When The Red Robin Went Bobbing Along

Dear Father Simon and the Gathered Forgivage,

A great weight has lain upon my chest since the summer of 1989 when I was the manager of a DIY store in the north of England. Please hear my sin.

Every morning my assistant manager, Ryan, and I would arrive at the store slightly early to wake up the computers and ready ourselves for the day ahead. Once preparations were done, we would sit down for a quick coffee before the chaos of the day set in. The office where this brief respite took place was on an upper floor of the building and had a window that overlooked the staff car park; this was particularly useful as we could witness the arrival of the rest of the store staff as we relaxed.

Almost without exception, Karen, one of the section managers, was the first to arrive. Day after day, week after week, we watched as she coaxed her small red Reliant Robin into a space to our right – but, oddly, she only ever came to a complete stop once she had bumped the front wheel up against the small kerb that bordered the car park.

We watched this process unquestioningly for many weeks. Each day the same manoeuvre took place: a sharp turn into the space, a burst of acceleration and the little car would surge forwards, stopping only when it came into contact with the solid stone kerb.

One dark morning, while nursing his steaming cup of coffee and watching the familiar routine of Karen's arrival, Ryan said, 'I wonder what would happen if someone moved that kerb?'

We both stopped what we were doing, our eyes met and nothing more needed to be said. A smile crossed our lips; a plan was hatched!

Within fifteen minutes of close of business that night, we had hauled out the solid stone kerb in front of Karen's space and replaced it with a strip of grey polystyrene, which we had selected from the warehouse. We then headed home eagerly.

Next morning, Ryan and I arrived as normal. We fired up the computers, got ourselves a coffee and positioned ourselves expectantly at the office window. Sure enough, bang on time, Karen appeared on the horizon. The little red Reliant Robin glinted in the morning sun as it glided gracefully across the car park towards her usual spot. She made her well-rehearsed turn and added the final burst of acceleration. The little car obediently jumped forward towards the expected, but absent, kerb . . .

Father Simon, I fear I require forgiveness from several parties here.

First, obviously, from Karen herself, who was waiting for the kerbside bump that didn't come and proceeded to direct her Reliant Robin, which frankly had more power than we'd given it credit for, off the edge of the car park, through a fence at the edge of the grounds, down the grassy verge and directly into the river that ran alongside the store.

Secondly, I feel I should spare a thought for the AA

man who had to call another AA man because the van he'd brought wasn't big enough to pull the Reliant back up the hill out of the river.

But thirdly, and most importantly, I must seek absolution from the horrified fisherman, who was just sitting on his basket that quiet summer morning, minding his own business. He ran like I have never seen a man run before, as he mercifully spotted the Reliant heading down the verge towards him at some speed, eventually ploughing straight through his equipment and basket on its way to its watery halt . . .

Can you possibly find it in your hearts to absolve me and Ryan of our sin?

Graham

PS We never did find the fisherman's basket.

Musical Differences

Dear Simon and the Forgiving Souls of the Confessional Collective,

My misdemeanour took place quite recently, so some of the details are a little sketchy (to protect the guilty), but I feel I must get it off my chest. I've played bass guitar in various local bands for a couple of years now. You know, belting out 'Mustang Sally', 'Sweet Home Alabama' and the like in pubs and clubs on a Saturday evening. All good clean fun and it keeps me off the streets.

However, in one particular band the fun was, sadly, missing. Now, I'm going to make a sweeping generalization about lead guitarists and say that they are all self-obsessed egomaniacs who never listen to anyone else, are never at fault and think the rest of the band should bow down in the face of their magnificence. In this band the guitarist – let's call him Jimmy – not only lived up to this stereotype, but had two additional, very annoying, habits. First, he always had, even in the smallest pub, a huge array of effects pedals laid out on the floor in front of him that would take up half the stage.

Honestly, Simon, I reckon spaceships have fewer buttons and switches. This, claimed Jimmy, was necessary for him to get the perfect sound for each song.

Secondly, Jimmy was always mysteriously absent when we were setting up before, and packing away after, gigs. You would be surprised by the amount of stuff even a small band carries around. Normally everyone mucks in and shares the load, but not Jimmy. 'Er, sorry I'm late, oh I see you've already set up' and 'Sorry, guys, can't help clear away tonight, must dash, I'm meeting someone' were typical excuses.

As you can imagine, our Jimmy was not the most popular of people. At one gig he then topped this off by blaming the drummer for a mistake he had clearly made himself. Enough was enough –

I decided a little retribution was in order, and so turned my attention to his beloved effects pedals.

In order to prompt him as to which of the umpteen buttons to press, he had a sheet of paper for each song, detailing the precise settings and the opening chords. These sheets were held in a ring binder, arranged in the order we had previously agreed we would play our set. During a mid-gig interval, Jimmy wandered off, and I saw my opportunity. It was only a few moments' work to rearrange these sheets into a new, and very different, order.

So, our break over, we got ready to start the second set. Bass, drums, keyboards and singer launched into 'Rock Around the Clock'. Jimmy, however, started playing 'Roll Over Beethoven'. It didn't sound good. Cue much confusion on Jimmy's part, and much sniggering from the rest of us. It was a similar scenario for the second song – as instead of 'Smoke On The Water', we played 'Crocodile Rock'. Next up, as Jimmy's baffled face grew redder, we launched into a lengthy 'Hotel California' and not the expected 'All Right Now'. By then, Jimmy had worked out that something was wrong and insisted we announce the songs before playing them, but that meant additional embarrassment for him as he had to frantically search through the ring binder looking for the song, while being heckled by the now bemused audience who had developed a very low opinion of his prowess. It was not one of our best gigs, and it left Jimmy looking, as he thumbed his way through the file, more like a nervy office clerk than a hedonistic rock 'n' roll axeman.

So I seek, nay beg, your forgiveness, not on behalf of Jimmy, who deserved everything he got; nor my fellow band members, who would have done the same if I hadn't got there first; but for the people in the audience, who must have wondered what on earth was going on, listening to a band who obviously found it hugely amusing that their guitar player was totally incompetent.

Funnily enough, Jimmy and I have never played together since.

Anon

Engine Trouble

Simon,

My confession dates back to a humid, warm and heavily overcast evening in August 1977, on the edge of a vast English moor. Picture the scene: there was no natural light at all, and only one artificial source – my motorcycle headlamp. I was out on the moor enjoying a ride on my first, and very noisy, large bike, a Ducati 750 V twin. Suddenly, my headlight failed. I brought the bike to a rapid halt and discovered the light fuse had blown, and not for the first time.

Being a well-prepared sort of a motorcyclist, I had a replacement fuse with me and set about changing it, but the job had to be done in total darkness. It wasn't easy, but I managed it, and I was about to start the bike up again when I heard young voices approaching. This place is known as a spooky area, even in daylight, and clearly the group of lads were a bit on edge and were teasing each other with creepy *woooooooooh* noises.

At this point, instead of turning my light back on and continuing my journey, I decided to play a little trick. I sat on the bike, unmoving and in total silence, and waited for them to get close. At that moment I started the machine and cranked up the maximum revs repeatedly, and added to the fright by screaming and howling like a moorland banshee. Then I turned the engine off and just as quickly fell silent.

The result was instant. They ran, shouting and yelling in fear, one even suggesting they turn off their torch so that 'it' couldn't see them. They kept running, totally panicked, until I couldn't hear them any more. I waited for several more minutes before restarting the bike and moving off – with a smug grin on my face. They had been totally spooked by my admittedly impressive, ghostly, nocturnal Evel Knievel nightmare effect.

Obviously, if I'd known they'd get lost on the moor overnight and have to be rescued, I wouldn't have done it.

I beg forgiveness for my sin and apologize, somewhat belatedly, to my victims, who must, at least for a while, have been traumatized.

Mick

Inch By Inch

Dear Father Simon, Brother and Sisters,

My confession is for an incident that occurred in 2008 and serves as an example of how, no matter how *short* a lie may be, it can cause anguish to people far, far away.

A friend of mine, let's call her Sarah-Jessica, was going on holiday to New York. Sarah-Jessica is a trusting soul and had previously asked me for advice in other areas, on all manner of topics, and had no cause to complain. Since I had been to New York, I was sought out for my opinion once more, and I offered some sound suggestions.

At the time, I'm sure you remember, the pound was very strong against the dollar, so shopping featured heavily on her 'To do' list. For reasons which, to this day, I am unable to explain, I decided to offer her a word of 'caution'. I told her to be particularly careful when buying clothes, because an American inch is *longer* than a British inch.

Like any normal person, she told me to stop being silly. And so, like any normal person, I mercilessly persisted with my ruse.

'It's true,' I said. 'You might buy a 32 and find that it's the equivalent of a 34. You know, because of the inches thing . . .'

I went on to explain that in the olden times, the measurement of a foot, and the 12 inches it contained, varied greatly until it was standardized by a wise and goodly king – I couldn't remember which one because it was a long time ago and, also, it never happened.

However, this regal clarification took place *after* the first settlers had reached America, meaning the difference in measuring a foot, and therefore an inch, had been preserved by the Atlantic Ocean. Despite the enormous historical problems with this explanation, I could see her slowly coming round, so I decided to press home my advantage and add some mortar to the brickwork of my lie.

'And it's not just inches,' I announced. 'A billion in America is different to a billion in the UK.' By chance, at precisely this moment, a friend joined us and confirmed that indeed a billion is different depending on which side of the pond you are. Sarah-Jessica thanked me kindly for my top tip and set sail for the New World.

I eventually learnt, from friends who were still speaking to me, that while trying to buy some clothes in an American store, Sarah-Jessica had asked the seemingly sensible question of what the equivalent UK inch size was. The shop assistant informed her that inches were the same all over the world.

Furious at the possibility of being conned into buying clothes that were too big for her, Sarah-Jessica launched into a tirade. The details of what followed are hazy and even eyewitnesses still disagree, but security was definitely called and Sarah-Jessica was definitely asked to leave.

Father Simon, I do not ask for forgiveness for my lie as it was so far-fetched and transparent that the most cursory piece of internet research would have disproved it instantly. Nor do I ask for forgiveness for betraying her trust. I am not even interested in forgiveness for blotting what was otherwise a perfect holiday.

I ask for forgiveness for having caused a shop assistant, who believed she was being helpful and informative, to endure all the shouting and the crying. And who to this day doesn't understand why a UK inch is any different to an American one.

Frank

An Electrifying Experience

Dear Simon and Team,

I think the time has come for me to publicly admit something I did more than twenty years ago. It still makes me titter when I think about it, and even though the victim of my prank is now aware, I think maybe I need forgiveness on a larger scale.

In the spring of 1989 I was studying at a university in Ireland. I shared a house with three other students; let's call them Karen, Elaine and Peter. The house was right on the coast, the bedrooms overlooked the sea and there was only a road between us and the view of the horizon. It was a lovely location.

Being fairly local, Karen, Elaine and I visited our families regularly, taking with us, as you do when you are a student, our washing. We returned with clean sets of clothes and bedding on an almost weekly basis. If for some reason we didn't go home, we'd use the launderette on the university campus.

Peter, however, whose family lived much further away, only went home when the term finished. He didn't have the same opportunity to get his washing done, but neither did he seem able to locate the campus launderette.

Us girls were horrified at his lack of cleanliness – sheets not changed for months at a time, using the same towel for weeks on end, YUK! When he found a girlfriend and she started to come and visit, we felt sure he would clean up his act, but no, that poor girl had to share his unwashed bed. We were simply appalled!

It was at this point that we decided Peter needed a

lesson in hygiene, and I have to admit to being the ringleader in this devious plan. I bought some itching powder from the small joke shop in the local town, and then we waited for an opportunity to present itself.

We didn't have to wait long. A couple of nights later he went off to the library to study for the evening, and as soon as the front door was closed, we converged on his bedroom and started to sprinkle itching powder on his sheets, pillows and duvet.

Our thinking was that if he itched, he would think it was because his sheets were dirty and he'd finally give them a wash. When we'd finished with the bed we thought, why stop here?, and so we liberally sprinkled powder through his underpants and sock drawers, just for good measure – after all, there was loads left, and it seemed a shame to waste it.

That night there was a tremendous electrical storm out over the sea. We watched the lightning with wonder, never having seen anything quite like it before. The next day Peter arrived at the breakfast table complaining of an odd feeling on his skin, and gradually he grew convinced that he had in some way become electrically charged during the night as a result of the storm.

We howled (inwardly) but went along with his theory, suggesting that the next time he was in the library he look into it.

For the next week he went around campus telling anyone who would listen that static electricity had taken over his body and generally making a fool of himself. After a few days the effects started to wear off, but as we still had lots of the powder left and the outcome had been so hilarious we decided to repeat the deed. This went on for a month or so. We all continued to marvel at the erratic and transient effects of static electricity on the human body, until we eventually thought we should stop and concentrate on our exams. The entertainment was over.

I should say at this stage that at no time did the sheets get a wash, so ultimately our plan failed, but it did give us and most of the university campus endless amusement at Peter's expense.

At the end of term, when we were celebrating finishing our exams, we finally broke it very gently to Peter that he had not been a scientific phenomenon nor been engulfed by static electricity, but merely the victim of common itching powder. He said nothing, but for the rest of the night I wore, with some pride, the remains of the pint he had been holding at the time.

Ironically, several months later when I'd left university and was getting married, my three housemates turned up, not unexpectedly, at my wedding, bringing with them gifts. Peter's contribution to my big day? Why, a laundry basket, of course!

Peter never did say whether or not he forgave me so I'm now asking you. Can I be forgiven for my deed?

Melanie

Tougher Than The Guest

Dear Father Simon, Mother Superior, and the superior intellect of the Collective,

Many years ago, as a twenty-year-old, semi-educated scruff, I was fortunate enough to be promoted to works manager of a company that specialized in the conversion of paper and plastics, for various trades.

These were ground-breaking times. One of the products new on the market was a material which, in the form we received it, was a white bonded fibre, with the appearance and feel of paper. In fact, any of you who have marvelled at the strength of some of the envelopes that documents are carried in by couriers will be familiar with this tough substance. Basically, you couldn't tear it, unless you cut or snagged the edge, and even then it was a struggle. And it looked just like paper.

One of our customers asked us to supply a large amount of this material for use by a building firm. It was to be used under roof tiles, in place of traditional under-felt. This is because it was a light, breathable membrane, waterproof, and could be printed on by building companies if desired, to undermine the efforts of the 'light-fingered'. At the end of the job, it was down to us to dispose of the unused sections responsibly.

Anyway, around that time, I received an invitation to an ex-girlfriend's wedding, to which I replied that I would be pleased to go. A group of my good friends were also going, so an enjoyable afternoon and evening would be had by all.

Being a responsible employee, the morning of the wedding I called in to work and rescued one of the written-off sections of material, dropped it on to the guillotine and cut it into exact lengths of 111mm (or, for those who prefer, 4 and ⅜ inches). I wound the newly cut material back on to a number of small cardboard reels and hid them in my bag, for reasons that will soon become clear.

I took my bag off to the church, where the wedding went perfectly and the bride looked great. Although it was a bit of a rush, my best friend (let's call him Mick) and I got to the reception first and raced in, charging through the doors of the ladies' and gents'. We exchanged every single toilet roll with our specially guillotined rolls of impenetrable paper-like material. We then left the scene and innocently took our place among the other guests, welcoming the happy, newly married couple.

Well, the temptation was too great. As soon as there was a twitch of the gents' door, we had to excuse ourselves and, standing where boys stand, listen to the rustling of paper and the horrified exclamations and general sounds of confusion coming from inside the cubicles. I was in constant tears. Honestly, Simon, I have never cried so much.

Father Simon, I beg the forgiveness of the following:

To those who spent ages in cubicles nibbling the edge of the paper to get it to tear. To the little old lady who, upon returning to the dining tables, declared she had had to sacrifice an expensive silk handkerchief.

And to the bride and groom, who, for a while, were not the number-one topic of conversation, and who stalled their car four times as I had looped a couple of strips of this evil material round their axle and connected it to the nearest lamp-post.

There you have it. I suppose I have to throw in that not only do I beg forgiveness for the deed itself, but also for the many times I have dined out on this story.

Geoff

All Mouth and No Trousers

Dear Father Simon,

I was a second chef in a very busy four-star hotel in a popular holiday town back in the 1960s and often played jokes on the other staff, such as removing the light bulbs from the female toilet cubicles, filling their umbrellas up with sugar and stapling up the other chefs' outdoor clothes so they were fighting to get their trousers on when it was time to go home.

As well as being a joker, I was always a bit of a ladies' man and, like an unreformed Sid James *Carry On* character (popular at the time), tried my luck with all the new waitresses who joined our team. I did manage to get a lot of dates over the months, but none of them resulted in long-lasting relationships. One morning a new waitress called Laura arrived for her induction. She was stunning, with long blonde hair and long legs. I told the other chefs to keep clear as she was going to be mine. Well, this was the 1960s, remember. And so I began the pursuit. In my civvies, I was actually a cool Mod, buying my clothes in Carnaby Street and the proud owner of a top-of-the-range silver Vespa scooter, but, of course, she didn't see any of this – only my boring chef's whites.

Well, hard as I tried, Laura repeatedly turned down my offers of a drink, going to the pictures and even going out for dinner. One evening, we had to call on the services of a relief chef, who seemed, to say the least, very attractive to the ladies. He was young, lithe and handsome. He also had a car, which I didn't.

During the first food service, he said to me, 'I've got a date with that hot young chick Laura – what do you think?'

What did I think? Well, it was unrepeatable! They flirted their way all through the shift, with me getting more and more hot under my collar with utter jealousy. All the time he was working, he was casually slurping on a can of cherry cola, which seemed to impress her. Halfway through the shift, however, he went to the toilet, and I had an evil idea. I found a bottle of red food colouring in the larder and emptied every last drop of it into his half-full drink can. He came back and continued through to the end of his shift, none the wiser.

Well, Father Simon, I have to say that my last vision of him that day was in the mirror of the changing room screaming, 'How can I go out with Laura tonight – my teeth are bleeding!' Yes, this beautiful red coloration not only ruined his chances of romance that night, but remained on his teeth for the next three days. (To add insult to injury, I told the hotel manager he really wasn't up to scratch and should be sent back to the agency whence he came.) He never did get to go out with Laura, although neither did I – she eventually went off with the hotel manager, no less.

Father Simon and all, please grant me forgiveness as I cannot even look at the red food colouring in the larder without recalling this terrible deed.

Bill

Ticket to Slide

Simon,

Many years ago, back in the 1960s, my local football club was doing very well in its league, so well that we had only one rival for the coveted league champions spot. All season the two clubs had jockeyed for position and now, nearing the end, they were at last to meet in what was billed as the match of the year, with the winner probably being crowned champion. It had been decided that the match would be an all-ticket affair and that tickets would go on sale the week before at a reserve match. For a 12-year-old schoolboy, the excitement was unbelievable. My friends and I decided to get to the ground early to beat the queue and help ensure we got our hands on the precious tickets.

The day arrived and we got to the ground at 11 a.m., only to find a queue of people far exceeding anything we had imagined. We were simply miles away from the turn-stiles. However, with a great deal of determination and resolution, we joined the queue and began the slow, torturous shuffle.

For over an hour we had hardly moved. The crowd was in a somewhat festive mood, however, and a fair bit of harmless banter was directed at the brave souls of the local constabulary as they policed the large gathering. This banter was particularly directed at one policeman who walked up and down the line of waiting fans with what can only be described as a waddle. As he waddled past us we couldn't resist whistling the Laurel and Hardy theme. You know the one. It was soon taken up by most of the crowd and it became apparent that the copper was finding it a little irksome – particularly as everyone stopped when he looked around to find who was doing it. This kept us amused for some time until hunger set in. My mother, a caring soul, had packed me a small lunch consisting of sandwiches, crisps and fruit. As we slowly shuffled along, I munched away happily.

It was a sudden surge in the crowd that threw us forward and made me drop the remains of my lunch, amongst which was a banana skin, that got kicked by the crowd into the middle of the pavement where the policeman was walking.

Like two forces of nature, the heel of waddling copper struck banana skin, resulting in possibly the greatest demonstration of inertia v. gravity ever witnessed. His legs shot from under him, his arms windmilled, his helmet parted company with his head and he landed in an undignified position on his back in the gutter. All this happened in a flash but I remember it as if it was in slow motion. The sharp intake of breath from the watching crowd was audible, shortly followed by an immense roar of laughter, further followed by the uncontrollable shaking of barely suppressed giggles as the PC struggled to his feet and cast his eyes about looking for the culprit. I, at this stage, realized the enormity of the situation and blended into the background like a big coward.

As the queue had moved on since I dropped the offending item, the policeman hauled out of the line the teenager who was closest and bundled him into the back of a nearby police van, which then sped away.

Simon, I have much to confess here, and I hope you will be benevolent and understanding. First, I apologize to and seek redemption from the poor policeman who bore the brunt of such childish humour. Secondly I seek redemption for the unmerited arrest of an innocent individual who probably spent the night in the local nick, didn't get a ticket and consequently missed the big match. Thirdly I apologize for being such a litterbug, for surely none of this would have happened had I been more careful with my lunch detritus. And fourthly I seek forgiveness for supporting a team that has over many years tried my patience to the full – and indeed perhaps that is punishment in itself. Father Simon, I await your admonishment, but please be merciful as I have carried these sins with me for a long time.

Phil

Even Letter Than The Real Thing

Simon,

For some considerable time now, I have been haunted by a past misdemeanour. I am worried that, when my time comes, I will be refused entry at the Pearly Gates. After much contemplation, I have decided to use your programme to confess all – not that I am about to depart this world yet, you understand.

You see, some thirty-odd years ago, my new young husband and I were invited to the wedding of one of his closest old school friends. The afternoon reception went all very well but halfway into the evening he got bored, and we decided to make a quick getaway when no one was looking. Soon afterwards, we moved to the West Country and my husband lost touch with his 'good friend'. Let's call the friend Paul, and let's call my husband Jeremy.

The years went by, but Jeremy always felt guilty about 'bunking off' from Paul's wedding. Then, unexpectedly, one Christmas, he received a card from Paul, who had managed to track him down via family from our home town. Jeremy was filled with guilt yet again, but as Paul did not include his address, Jeremy was unable to contact him.

The following Christmas came another card. It was bad news: Paul and his wife had split up. The year after, yet another card – this time Paul had lost his job. Oh, the sorrow! A year later and, yes, another festive card appeared on the doormat. This time, Paul had been rather ill. Skip forward a year, and Paul had now lost his house. Another year, and we learned that he had called in on us whilst visiting the West Country but, unfortunately, we'd been out. Jeremy was so sad to have missed his friend. The Christmas cards kept coming, but always bearing yet more news of Paul's misfortune.

Then, those websites were formed – you know, the ones where you can get in touch with old friends – and Jeremy wondered if he would finally be able to make contact. I was HORRIFIED and, mysteriously, the Christmas cards dried up.

So, here comes my confession! I'm so glad to get it off my chest. I love my husband dearly but he listens to this programme and I'm not sure how he will react. You see, many years ago, knowing how guilty he was feeling at slinking off from his friend's wedding, I decided – just for a laugh, you understand – to fake a Christmas card from Paul. Of course, Jeremy would recognize my handwriting and the joke would be over in a matter of moments. But imagine my surprise when Jeremy took this card to be genuine. Simon, he fell for it, hook, line and sinker. Wicked thoughts along the lines of 'Oh, this is too good to be true' popped into my head.

So, of course, the following year, just in case he'd recognize my handwriting this time, I asked our neighbours to write Paul's name. And then, afraid he might notice the local postmark, I sent Paul's fake card to family members still living in our old home town, where Jeremy believed Paul still to be residing, for them to post back to our house.

Jeremy, I love you dearly, but will you still love me when you hear that there were never any cards from Paul – they all came from me, and, what's more, our family and neighbours have been in on the joke for all these years. I haven't even got the guts to tell you face to face. Darling Jeremy, please, please forgive me!

Mary

Clergy

Some of my best friends are Reverends. They are decent, humorous and more-or-less normal people. There is still, however, something undeniably comical about 'the vicar' and for this I blame Derek Nimmo and Frank Williams. Nimmo was a regularly wet TV holy man, *Oh, Brother* and *All Gas And Gaiters* setting the benchmark. Williams was the clueless Rev Timothy Farthing in *Dad's Army*. Then came *Father Ted* and the conclusion was unavoidable; if you want an instant comedy moment, call for the vicar.

Blessing in Disguise

Dear Simon and the Confessional,

I am a good Catholic girl and I would like finally to confess to a shameful deed.

In 1983 I and four other severely deaf children, all aged around twelve, went from Dublin to Lourdes to see Pope John Paul II. It took two days to get there by coach. The day after arrival, we went to Lourdes Grotto to see the Pope. We had been selected to be blessed by the Holy Father.

We were arranged in different disability groups and I was at the start of the line of deaf people, positioned next to the wheelchair group. The blessing was to take place in the mid-afternoon, but we'd had to make an early start and do a lot of waiting around. This, on top of our marathon journey to get there, meant we were very tired. Next to me was a spare wheelchair, beside a girl in her own wheelchair. Exhausted, I couldn't resist, so I sat down. I began chatting to the other girl and she explained she had two broken legs. She asked me what had happened to me. I told her there was nothing wrong with my legs, it was just my ears.

All at once the Pope arrived, it was our turn, and I was firmly told by the officials *not to move*. The Pope moved along the line, giving everyone a blessing. I told the girl, 'Oh God, I hope he's not blessing my legs, I want my ears blessed!' She wished me good luck.

Then I got my blessing. Wow! Pope John Paul II, what a nice man he was. Afterwards, happy and excited, I wheeled myself along the road with my new friend and we decided, as kids do, to have a race. We counted to three and set off. After a couple of wheel turns, I got a little carried away, jumped up out of the chair and ran, because I really wanted to win. I had forgotten where we were and what we were there for. Suddenly there was pandemonium all around.

A French copper, resplendent in his uniform, looked on open-jawed and declared it to be a miracle. 'Bless the Pope!' he exclaimed. People began asking me for my autograph and having their pictures taken with me, and I did absolutely nothing to stop them. My mother was mortified, and I was told, in no uncertain terms, to get back in the chair and stay there for the evening mass.

I still haven't had the nerve to confess to this in church. So, Simon and the Confessional Collective, I now beg the forgiveness of the late Pope, no less, and of all who witnessed my actions, especially the French policeman, who thought he had seen a miracle, and probably still thinks he did. Even to this day I have the photo of the two of us together in Lourdes.

Oh, and I'm still deaf, so no change there . . .

Kellie

The Graveyard Shift

Father Simon,

I have listened to many confessions on your programme and feel that it is now my turn. It's the only way to purge myself of the guilt of what happened all those years ago.

I cannot say who I am other than that in 1993 I was a newly ordained Anglican priest who also worked as a police officer in an isolated moorland town. The church where I served was in the centre of the town, where it had stood for nearly a thousand years. It was surrounded by beautiful cottages, and peace and quiet reigned – that is, until a group of teenagers began to frequent the steps of the church late at night. One of my elderly parishioners complained she was being kept awake by the yobs drinking cans of beer. She also felt quite frightened, and asked me to pray alongside her that God would sort out the problem. Simon, this happened to coincide with me, in my role as policeman, going on a few weeks of nights, but every time we tried to catch the youths, they always managed to disappear into the darkness of the churchyard, never to be caught. It happened over several weekends in the long hot summer of 1993. I prayed and prayed, asking God for advice. Eventually I was struck with an idea.

I spotted the group of seven youths at the top of the market-place, and I secretly returned to my house and collected my long white 'cassock alb' – a garment with long sleeves and a hood, normally worn by a monk. I arranged with my uniformed colleague that when I alerted him on his police radio, he should drive up to the church with lights flashing and siren wailing.

Night fell, and I could hear the youngsters carousing by the church steps. I got ready, and gave the signal. Far away I heard the siren and soon saw the blue flashing lights reflecting off the church tower. Then came the hurried footsteps of several burly, drunken teenagers, running into the churchyard to escape the police. In the pitch dark, clad in my alb, I rose up from behind a gravestone and began to wail. And, Simon, how I wailed. What they saw, in their highly inebriated condition, I can't say, but it certainly wasn't a policeman in a dress. All of them began to scream. The one nearest to me clutched his chest and began to wheeze in terror. Another whimpered, while a third petrified yob clutched his pathetic friend's sleeve for comfort.

For moments they stood there, frozen in fear. Then they ran. Leaping a six-foot stone wall, they made off across the gardens surrounding the church. They fell into the large fishpond of the manor house with a resounding splash and crashed through the greenhouse. Their screams rang out through the still summer night and echoed through the houses. For some reason I gave chase. It was enjoyable, sadistic and fulfilling. I was getting revenge for all the sleepless nights they had caused the old dear in the nearby cottage. I wailed like a hound from hell, their screams getting louder and louder. They must have thought the devil himself was pursuing them. Eventually I collapsed on the grass, laughing so much I could barely breathe. That said, it was wonderful.

From that night on they never came back, and the town returned to peace and quiet. The old woman thanked God for answering her prayers. As for what had really happened, the only clues were the tell-tale grass stains on my alb.

I left the police eventually. My colleague was promoted through the ranks to senior police officer. I still remember that night and the look of total and utter fear on the faces of those young lads, who thought they had come face to face with a demon from hell.

As a priest I cannot forgive myself for what I have done, but I hope you can.

Anon

The Holy Toast

Dear Father Mayo,

The incident in question occurred seventeen years ago when I was one of eighty training to be men of the cloth. It was about 6.30 a.m. on a cold and wet October day. I was eating my breakfast when a dear friend of mine walked in, the worse for wear after a good night out the evening before, and tiredly and a little rudely asked me to place some toast in the toaster for him. I asked him if he wanted toast in the toaster, to which he replied yes, so I did exactly as he asked, toasted some bread and placed it back in the toaster. I then left the dining room and headed for the shower.

Now, just a couple of months earlier, the fire alarm system in this illustrious institution had been updated, and just as I entered the shower, the fire alarms went off. Realizing that it must have been the re-toasted toast that set off the alarms, and that I was therefore responsible, I decided the safest thing was to remain in the shower, in hiding, while everybody else hurriedly interrupted their ablutions to exit the building.

I sneaked a look out of the window and saw that on the lawns were lines and lines of future clergymen at the fire evacuation assembly point, with nothing but the tiniest towels covering their modesty, shivering away. I then saw my dear friend walking out, holding the two offending slices of toast. His apologies were drowned out by the torrent of highly unbiblical abuse he received from the near naked throng of holy trainees and, for months later, whatever he said was replied to with a similar chorus.

And so I must seek forgiveness for my actions, but not from my dear friend. As a Tottenham supporter, he qualifies as a life-long member of the Association of Big Girl's Blouses, and, as their sole purpose in life is to receive abuse, he is merely fulfilling his destiny.

No, I must seek the forgiveness of all those shivering clergymen – who included at least two high-ranking archdeacons, a row of five or so right reverends in the making, and, if I'm not mistaken (it was a bit steamy through the bathroom window), a particularly red-faced future bishop, no less – as they did not ask for this kind of humiliation.

I do not think that you, Father Mayo, as another life-long member of the aforementioned association, will look too kindly upon this, and therefore I must rely upon the rest of the collective to bring common sense to the proceedings. From them, I humbly request absolution.

Richard

The Reverend Randy Lover

Dear Father Mayo and the Assembled Collective,

I have a very good friend, who also happens to be a man of the cloth, whom for the purposes of this confession we'll call Reverend Steve.

Reverend Steve has an obsession with Land Rovers. He talks about them endlessly, he uses them as sermon illustrations, he cannot drive past one without giving a detailed breakdown of its specification. In short he is a 'Landy' anorak.

Imagine, then, my joy in discovering that there was available a range of spoof Land Rover badges, made in the exact same style, font and logo as the one you would normally find on the vehicle. The one I set my heart on proclaimed not my friend's beloved automotive brand but instead the words 'Randy Lover'. I sent for one in the same colour as his vehicle and as soon as the opportunity presented itself I secretly glued it to the back door.

For the next month Reverend Steve drove around blissfully unaware of the stir he was causing.

Pedestrians would wave and cheer as he went by, cars behind him would sound their horns, and members of the public would give him very strange looks as he parked his pride and joy and emerged wearing his clerical collar – most especially at a couple of funerals he had to conduct.

It was only when a little old lady in his congregation berated him for his warped and inappropriate sense of humour and pointed out to him the offending badge that he realized what was happening.

Knowing I had something of a reputation for being a practical joker, he immediately accused me of blackening his good name. I, of course, robustly denied everything and even went on to say that carrying a badge saying 'Randy Lover' might enhance *his* reputation.

I could tell he wasn't convinced, and he was equally unhappy that it took him the best part of a day to remove the badge, so I suggested that a mutual friend of ours called Simon, a mechanic who regularly worked on both our vehicles, might have both motive and opportunity to carry out this heinous act of sabotage.

Surprisingly, he believed my story and confronted Simon, whose unfortunate predisposition towards blushing only seemed to confirm his guilt, in spite of his protestations to the contrary.

I subsequently moved out of the area, but before leaving, took the opportunity to do the same thing again with a second badge I had purchased at the time. The results were more or less identical and Reverend Steve was left with only his suspicions and a slightly tarnished image. I am not sure how much absolution I may get for leaving Simon in the frame, or for repeating my actions, but on the positive side, the references to Land Rovers did reduce for quite some time!

Mike

Defrocked

Simon,

This is a 'sin' of high order, which took place in one of the country's most beautiful cathedrals and in front of all the senior clergy of the Church of England.

Many years ago I was invited to the ordination of the new bishop of the city. The invitation was extended by the mother of a friend of mine, who is well known and well respected. The layout of the cathedral is somewhat unusual as the pews face inwards towards the aisle. It was a very, very hot sunny day. My friend's younger sister was seated next to me, nearest the aisle. My friend's mother was on my other side and my friend on her other side.

The atmosphere was solemn, and the congregation talked in hushed tones. Led by the Archbishop of Canterbury, the senior clergy of the Church of England made a magnificent entrance, dressed in all their ecclesiastical finery. They processed up the aisle to the mighty altar in a solemn line. During the ordination ceremony, the congregation sat quietly and respectfully in the pews. At the end, with the organ playing and again led by the archbishop, the procession came slowly back down the aisle. The protocol was that as the Archbishop of Canterbury came level with you, you stood up. (A bit like the Wembley wave.) Simon, the atmosphere was reverential.

As I said, it was a very hot day. My friend's younger sister was wearing a very attractive sundress. Without straps. And no jacket. The archbishop drew level with my friend's sister and she stood up a fraction before I did. Neither of us realized I had been sitting on her dress. The dress stayed where it was but she didn't, therefore revealing a lot more than she intended to the Archbishop of Canterbury and all the bishops in the land. As she found herself standing there topless, her 'Oh my God' rang out across the cathedral and caused the procession to come to an abrupt halt. The archbishop and bishops all sort of cannoned into each other (a bit of a religious play on words there) and turned and stared.

As my friend's sister tried desperately to regain her modesty by pulling her dress up, hissing at me out of the side of her mouth, the realization that I had been responsible began to permeate my consciousness.

The procession down the aisle started again, albeit a bit raggedly. We were supposed to be going to a reception afterwards to meet the newly ordained bishop, but for some reason it was decided this wouldn't be a good idea and I remember we left hurriedly out of a side entrance.

My friend's sister didn't speak to me for quite a while, but I hope I can now be forgiven.

Anonymous

Nudity

A special section. A choice few confessions feature full or partial nudity and might shock gentler readers. There is a dreamlike, or maybe nightmare-like, quality to these stories as more is revealed than we ever intended. While we might be ready for nakedness in movies and on TV, surprising, unplanned and, let's be honest, unwelcome expanses of flesh still have the power to embarrass. And amuse.

Darling, I'm Home

Simon,

A few years ago, I was living with my boyfriend in a top-floor flat which shared a small landing with the flat opposite. At that time my boyfriend was working abroad for two weeks out of four and, on this particular evening, he had phoned me from the airport, as was his habit, to tell me he'd be home soon. I had been busy with some flowerpots on the balcony and I was feeling a bit grubby. I hopped in the shower.

The doorbell went. It would not have been the first time my boyfriend had forgotten to take his keys with him, so I jumped out of the shower and threw open the door, expecting to see my forgetful partner and give him a good-natured telling off. It was, as I'm sure you're expecting by now, not him. It was, in fact, given my state of undress, the most unsuitable visitor you could possibly imagine – an elderly Jehovah's Witness, *Watchtower* in hand, who greeted me with something along the lines of 'Hello, have you thought about AAAARGH!' with an expression that indicated he had probably never seen a naked woman before, and that he'd really rather never see one again.

He disappeared off down the stairs at quite a rate, and, part way down, let out another horrified cry. I could hear a thumping from the stairwell and so assumed that this, now, would be my boyfriend, lugging his suitcase and, possibly, wearing a rather tasteless T-shirt that had caused further offence to the beleaguered religious chap. There didn't seem to be any point going back indoors for the thirty seconds it would take him to make it up the last flight of stairs, so I waited, still naked, dripping shampoo bubbles.

Unfortunately, the thumping noise wasn't my boyfriend either. It was the gentleman from the flat opposite, dragging a tartan shopping trolley with a missing wheel and, to my surprise, revealing a side to him I had not previously seen. He was wearing a green skirt-suit and a wig. I was so surprised by this – something I suppose explained the second shout from the stairs – that I didn't immediately close the door.

I have already been forgiven by my boyfriend for the rather frosty reception he got when he finally did get home, having been stuck in traffic for half an hour, so I would like to seek forgiveness, not so much from the Jehovah's Witness, because as my gran used to say, 'If you can see more than God made, throw your hat at it', but from the chap from the flat opposite, who was probably rather embarrassed by my suggesting that if he was going to wear sheer tights, he really ought to shave his legs.

Karen

A Right Royal Fright

Dear Simon,

When I was eighteen – I'm sixty-five now – I worked in a Cornish tin mine. It was 2,160 feet straight down, and at this depth underground, heat and humidity were high. On the day in question, I was set to work on what was called the Grizzly – a lot of reclaimed rails from British Rail, which together formed a criss-cross section over a sheer drop to the next level down and the crusher. My job as the 'Grizzly man' was to break up rocks – some of which weighed over a ton each – using a hefty 12- or 16-pound sledgehammer, and send them on their way down. Some of these rocks were so hard the sledge would bounce off them, so then dynamite had to be used. So there I was, breaking rocks, hungover from the night before because of a birthday party, suitably dressed for the job in hand – stark naked except for a helmet, battery belt and boots, due to the heat – and swearing a lot because I didn't seem able to break this one rock. The shift boss was nowhere to be found and I needed him to blast it with dynamite.

Then I heard the cage (a large metal lift) arrive at our level, and indistinct voices coming towards me. I continued swinging the sledgehammer and swearing every time it just bounced back with nothing more to show for my effort than a few chips and some dust. My back was turned towards the people arriving, but I assumed one of them was my shift boss, finally there to help me. As I turned to ask for explosives – and let me remind you of my demeanour here: I was naked and filthy from sweat and dirt – I was greeted with the unforgettable words, 'And this, your highness, is the Grizzly.' Yes, Simon, unknown to me, a VIP visitor was being shown around the mine. He was a young man back then, and more recently his son was married in Westminster Abbey – just to give you a hint as to his identity. He was there with his team and the top brass from the mine management. And me, completely starkers and grubby.

Time stood still, and in that moment all I could see was the glaring brightness from the special lights they were using for the visit, and lots of men in white boiler suits, but the laughter was infectious and I had to join in. The party went on their way and I went back to breaking rocks, and naturally I took a lot of stick in the showers later, but all in all the hangover was declared cured!

So I now seek forgiveness from the entire Windsor family, and any other members of the royal household and its staff who had the pleasure of meeting me that day. I especially beg the pardon of his royal highness himself, and I hope that the sight of a stinky foul-mouthed Cornishman in his birthday suit didn't traumatize our future King too much.

Jack

Better Trout Than In

Simon,

Hearing a recent confession, I was reminded of an incident that occurred to me some twenty-odd years ago, when I was invited to spend a week fishing on the river Spey.

I was enjoying myself, although I was catching more heather than fish. The days were civilized and well organized, with coffee breaks and biscuits. After my mug of coffee one especially fine morning, I returned to my assigned position on the river to see if anything would bite. In the normal way that all fluids – but, it seems to me, particularly coffee – work their way quite naturally through the system, I became aware of an increasing desire to relieve myself. I should mention that I was fishing with chest-high waders on, and to carry out the necessary bodily function the lowering of the waders to one's knees was required, involving elaborate unbuckling, unbuttoning and unfastening. Although the party was well spaced out and I could not see my neighbouring fisherfolk, I thought it would be more graceful to walk through the thin tree-line and turn my back on the riverbank in case anyone from my party should walk by, as it would take quite a bit of work to restore my dignity if spotted in the middle of doing what nature was calling for.

So, fit to burst, there I was, standing with my back to the river with these somewhat cumbersome wading boots round my knees, gazing across the beautiful view of Scottish fields. How lovely and idyllic. Having become fully committed to the relieving act, I was taken by surprise when a shiny green Range Rover appeared from nowhere, through some trees to my left, travelling along a track that ran parallel to the river, a track that had not been apparent to me through the heather. The vehicle was passing only yards from where I was standing, in full unstoppable flow, tethered at the knees by my half-undone waders. As the vehicle drew closer, and my face became redder and my bladder that bit emptier, I was unable to stop and unable to move. And so it came to pass that I unintentionally 'flashed' the future King of England and his wife as they slowly drove past.

I suspect it is relatively small, the club of people who have got away with baring all to royalty, but I'm happy, nay proud, to join the 65-year-old miner from Cornwall.

So, Father Simon and the Holy Trinity, I beg forgiveness for a sin that in years gone by might have meant a one-way trip to the Tower of London and the involuntary separation of one's head from one's shoulders. For while I had merely tried to prevent any embarrassment to my own party, I had caused acute embarrassment to myself and quite possibly the royal couple.

I was introduced to the prince some twenty-one years later, but he did not recognize me, possibly as I was fully clothed this time, and I thought it a subject best not brought up!

Angus

Brassed Off

Dear Father Simon and the Christmas Collective,

In the early 1990s I played in a well-respected brass band in the south-west of England. One night at practice there was an air of great excitement as the bandmaster announced we were to play a Christmas carol for a TV recording when the town's Christmas lights were switched on. This would be followed by our annual Christmas concert – the highlight of our banding year.

As the time for the recording approached, the temperature plummeted, and on the day itself I didn't relish the thought of standing in the cold for hours on end, shivering in my band uniform, just to record two minutes of 'Jingle Bells' for the TV. We were not allowed to wear coats, and because of the concert immediately after the TV recording, there was going to be no time to warm up in customary brass-band style (in the pub!). So I pulled on a pair of black leggings under my uniform skirt for warmth.

Simon, we played our hearts out, and finished with frozen valves on our instruments and frozen fingers. We then retreated to the relative warmth of the town hall for our concert. Before going on stage, I needed to remove the leggings. I didn't know the layout of the hall so I asked my best friend, also a member of the band, for directions to the loo. 'Top of the stairs, and turn left,' she said confidently. Time was short and I ran up the poorly lit staircase, turned left as advised and, fumbling around in the dark, opened the door into the room. With no time to lose, I hoicked up my skirt and started squirming around to remove the leggings. It was then that I heard a murmuring sound. Thinking that it was a strange noise to hear in the loo, I looked over my shoulder and realized I wasn't in the loo at all. I was standing on the balcony of the town hall, overlooking the massed audience, who were all in full view. I disappeared very quickly, found the loo, and later chastened my friend for sending me in the wrong direction. (Though she claims to this day that it was my inability to tell left from right, combined with the dim lighting, that caused the problem.) I'd like to apologize to the good people of the audience that night, who saw far more of their brass band than was good for them. Also to the conductor, who was blissfully unaware of what was unfolding on the balcony above him, as he ran through the programme one last time. At least I had put on my best pants that morning.

I'm still playing in a brass band and happily have not suffered any similar embarrassment since.

Holly

Northern Exposure

Dear Father Simon,

I write to unburden myself of a great feeling of guilt I have borne since the dark days of November 1982. I shudder every time my mind is drawn to that dreadful night in Yorkshire.

Let me explain. I was a twenty-year-old living in the south of England. My girlfriend, Glenda (now my wife of twenty-four years), and I decided on a mini-break to the north-west. As usual, such breaks tended to coincide with wherever Southampton Football Club happened to be playing. On this occasion it was a pilgrimage for the usual stuffing at Old Trafford (the mighty Saints in those days were known as 'Southampton Nil' – some things never change).

Anyway, our team having been summarily dismissed by the opposing side, Glenda and I travelled across the Pennines on a cold dark night to meet up with my sister and her husband at a hotel in Yorkshire. Arriving late, we settled in, then spent an enjoyable next day discovering the locality and doing the sorts of things you do at that age, namely shopping (the women) and eating and drinking (the boys).

Our hotel was a lovely old building with a roaring log fire and that night we decided to have a special evening in and a nice meal there, along with a few drinks. We thought we'd dress for dinner to make it really special. Thus the early evening was spent scrubbing up and getting ready for the feast ahead. This is where it all went a bit pear-shaped.

You see, our two rooms faced each other across the corridor and as the ladies got ready, there were frequent scurries from one room to the other to borrow bits and pieces (hairbrushes, safety pins, lippy) and of course to ask the inevitable questions ('Does my bum look big in this?' etc.).

Us chaps quickly tired of this game, which seemed to go on for hours, so we settled down in our respective rooms to watch the football scores roll in on the TV. About ten minutes before dinner I undressed and showered, while the better halves were still rushing back and forth 'preparing' for the night ahead.

There came the umpteenth knock at our bedroom door. By now slightly irritated by my sister's visits, I waited for the second knock, and as it went unanswered, I reluctantly shouted, 'I'll get it, then.' As it turned out, my future wife was fighting with the hairdryer and was oblivious to the knock.

I leapt purposely from the shower to greet my sister at the door. Flinging it open wide, and for special effect dropping the towel that was around my waist, I stood there in all my glory, arms in the air. 'Hang loose, big sis,' I shouted, with all I possessed now on full display.

What followed will live with me for ever. You see, it wasn't my sister standing in the doorway, neither was it my brother-in-law. Instead, frozen, eyes wide and face contorted in horror, stood a middle-aged, craggy waitress, notebook in hand, come to ask what we would like from the evening's menu.

Abjectly, I covered my intimate area as best I could (in what can only be described as a cartoon manner) and jumped back inside the room. 'GLENDA!' I shouted. 'Quick, there is a lady at the door asking what we want to eat – tell her I'll have anything!'

Totally oblivious to my misdemeanour, my future Mrs duly obliged and informed the waitress of our requirements. 'She was a bit miserable,' remarked Glenda as she returned, 'and she looked rather shocked.'

She certainly was, and there was no flicker of a smile that evening either as she served us at our table. In fact, she positively banged my meal down in front of me.

So, Father Simon and Collective, I now beg forgiveness. Not from my sister, who, on the occasion of my twenty-first a month later presented me with a silver tankard bearing the words 'Hang Loose'; nor from my wife-to-be, who found the whole thing hysterical, when the story was told. But from the good staff of the hotel, and in particular the craggy waitress, who may have been unable to deliver room service for the rest of her life. I place myself and my ill-judged actions at your mercy . . .

Jim

Making Quite A Splash

Dear Simon,

What I wish to confess happened a few years ago at a local hotel, one of a well-known chain, with a very nice leisure club attached to it.

Before this particular incident, my friend Mark and I used to visit our local leisure centre every Monday night for an hour's gym work. The leisure centre was located on the banks of a river and was prone to flooding, and after one very wet winter the centre was so seriously damaged the council decided to rebuild it. This was going to take at least a year, so users of the centre were offered preferential rates at the nearby hotel's leisure club in the meantime. Mark and I continued our Monday-night routine but using the hotel gym instead, an hour each week, a quick shower and then home promptly, especially Mark, whose wife worked nights.

One Monday, however, after our gym work had finished and I was having my shower, Mark came in and asked whether I'd join him for a swim afterwards as his wife wasn't working that particular evening. Having never used the hotel pool before, I agreed. I said I'd be in shortly.

I arrived at the poolside and noticed Mark standing at the far end but not yet in the water.

I walked right round the edge of the pool, past the collection of floats and water-wings, past the lengthy 'no petting' signage which I stopped to peruse, past the base of the lifeguard's lookout chair, past the large stopwatch and poolside thermometer, gradually acquainting myself with these unfamiliar surroundings. When I finally reached him, he greeted me only with the words, 'Sean – you haven't got any trunks on.' The change to our normal routine had caused me to forget myself, and I had walked straight from the shower into the pool area. By this time there was sniggering echoing all around the pool, which unfortunately alerted the lifeguard to my appearance. Like a schoolboy being caught splashing girls or dive-bombing, I was subjected to the full audible wrath of his official whistle and ordered to go and cover up or face removal or even a ban from the centre. I then had to walk back round the pool completely starkers to the changing rooms, covering what needed to be covered up with my hands, only to sheepishly reappear fully trunked a few moments later. It was truly, Simon, a walk of shame.

I therefore beg the forgiveness of the many people using the pool that night who were subjected to the sight of me in all my glory. I would also like to ask Mark to assume some responsibility on the basis that he let me walk the entire length of the pool (which was of Olympic size, as I recall) before informing me of my wardrobe malfunction.

Sean

Bathing in Glory

Dear Simon and the Confessions Crew,

Hearing the tale of the young man who unintentionally walked out starkers at a public swimming pool, I feel the time is right to confess to my own moment of shame.

A number of years ago, I went on a business trip with a colleague to Oslo. The flight was supposed to have left from London at 9 a.m., but thanks to mechanical problems and general British efficiency, it did not take off for twelve hours, meaning we didn't reach Oslo until near enough midnight.

After a fraught taxi ride through a snow storm, we arrived bleary-eyed at our hotel with its very bright blue lobby and checked in. On the way to our rooms, we noticed a huge pool, steam floating above the water: it looked very inviting indeed after such a horrible day. However, neither of us had swimming trunks . . . but it was so late, absolutely no one else was around, and we thought, why not? We ran into the pool area, stripped down to our birthday suits and jumped into the warm, inviting pool. It was bliss after all our tribulations.

We swam to the deep end, which was strangely lit from behind along its entire width, curious as to what that was all about. When we got there, we discovered why the illumination was so bright, as well as why the hotel lobby was blue. Yes, Simon, the entire end wall of the pool was made of glass and it faced directly into the lobby itself.

Now, this wouldn't have been so bad at such a late hour, except that at that very moment, two coach-loads of pensioners had arrived at the hotel and were checking in – their journeys perhaps delayed by the snow storm – only to be greeted by the sight of two naked men floating behind the reception desk. I'm not sure who was more surprised when we saw each other, but I do know we moved a lot faster – well, as fast as one can while underwater, especially if forced to use one hand for protecting one's modesty rather than swimming.

Back at the other end, we jumped out of the pool and ran back to our rooms, and hoped we wouldn't be thrown out into the cold. Luckily the hotel staff were of an understanding nature, but the next morning at breakfast, we were given quite a few odd glances by the pensioners, to say the least. I'm afraid I milked it a bit at the buffet, standing next to two elderly ladies and smiling and winking at them.

So I'd like to ask the forgiveness of a hundred Scandinavian septuagenarians for the unexpected appearance of two naked divers, and hope their trip wasn't ruined by the experience.

Yours floating in anticipation, John

Animals

In the long distant 1990s, some of the most famous confessions appeared in this section. Goats, hamsters and mice became the star turn. This time round it's the turn of fish, lovebirds and chinchillas. But the human story is always the same . . .

You Can't Teach Some Dogs Any Tricks

Dear Father Simon and the Collective,

I write to seek forgiveness for something that occurred many years ago when I was about fourteen.

After an incident in which our family dog Clara, a young and playful Alsatian, got hold of a wallet of cash (another story for another time), it was decided some training would be useful. We quickly found the ideal candidate, an ex-police dog trainer with a 100 per cent success rate, who specialized in Alsatians. Classes were held once a week in a large local park.

Clara was a very bright dog. In fact, within our family there was a general belief that she was beyond obedience, that she knew exactly what to do but chose to ignore it.

Nevertheless I dutifully attended with her on a regular basis, took part in the lesson and handed over my money to the instructor at the end. I listened carefully and tried my hardest to manipulate Clara into displaying some kind of obedience, like the other well-behaved dogs in the group. But it was to no avail.

A clue that our training was not going well was probably the point at which the rest of the class started to have lessons without me. Another clue came when the dog previously accepted as the worst behaved in the group came and stood near us and resembled a Cruft's obedience champion by comparison. It wasn't long before the lessons – those from which we weren't excluded – consisted of about 20 per cent training and 80 per cent restraining efforts on the part of the instructor.

One of the warm-up exercises we all did was making the dog sit down, removing the lead and walking slowly away, as far as you felt comfortable, before returning to praise your pet for remaining in place. Knowing Clara, I had decided long ago that trusting her in this way would be a mistake, so while the trainer's gaze was elsewhere I would leave the lead in place and stand firmly on its end. On the fateful day he noticed what I was doing and came over to tell me my approach was all wrong. He took my place, removed Clara's lead, got her sitting and told her to stay, then walked away. In the meantime, the rest of the class continued the exercise with the other canine participants.

Clara looked at the instructor, looked at me, looked at the now released lead, and with a loud happy bark ran off into the distance – much as I had expected she would. What came as a surprise, however, was that she was quickly followed by the rest of the obedience dogs, in what began to resemble a Red Arrows attack formation flying at speed across the park. Now, normally the park in which we practised didn't have much going on. But on this particular occasion they were setting up for the County Show, due to take place the following day. So there was quite an audience, not to mention tents and ropes and all manner of places to 'mark territory' and, frankly, hide.

The once obedient dogs relished their new-found freedom, running here, there and everywhere. For the next two hours, owners and workmen alike roamed the field, shouting and clapping and trying to get all the dogs to return. My sister eventually arrived to collect Clara and me, exactly at the point when the police dog unit turned up to try to resolve the situation (much to the embarrassment of the ex-police dog trainer). Clara, spotting my sister, ran up to greet her and jumped in the car without hesitation. At this point I had to go and pay the instructor. I will not repeat what he said to me.

Suffice to say, Clara was expelled from dog obedience class forthwith.

I don't seek forgiveness from the instructor, as I feel misled by his '100 per cent success rate' claim and was stung by his parting words. I don't seek forgiveness from the other participants, as I am sure the exercise did the dogs good and anyway they shouldn't have left us out of the other classes. I don't seek forgiveness from the people who were setting up for the County Show, as they had a very good laugh. I do, however, think I should seek forgiveness from the police, who were obliged to turn up and help to catch the dogs. Although, to be fair, the police station was very near the park and it did take them two hours to get there.

So, can you forgive the owner of a badly behaved dog who has long departed this earth?

Sarah

Time to Own Op

Simon,

Five years ago, my husband and I got an adorable male Labrador-collie puppy. All went well and the whole family fell in love with him. But when he was a year old, the hormones kicked in and he started to show an interest in roaming. The children got very upset if he went missing for any length of time. Also, when any female canine friends came around, he'd be very amorous with them, much to my boys' amusement.

So I broached the subject of a trip to the vet and a small operation to sort out these 'problems'. Well, to say my husband objected would be an understatement. From his reaction you'd have thought I was suggesting *him* for the op instead. 'No dog of mine is having *that* done!' he said firmly. There was to be no more discussion . . .

However, one day he announced he was going away on a short business trip. I'd had a particularly stressful time dealing with our 'teenage' dog, so I made a small deal with myself: if I rang up the vet's and they had a space, he would be in – if not, then it was not meant to be. Well, Simon, they had a space. The day arrived and my husband left at 6 a.m. for the airport. I left for the vet's at 8 a.m. I explained the situation and asked if they could use internal stitches and not shave his leg if at all possible (for the anaesthetic). They agreed. I picked up a rather dozy dog in the afternoon who had a shaved tummy and, obviously, other alterations to his appearance.

My eldest, who was ten at the time, noticed immediately, so I explained that we needed to keep it a secret otherwise Daddy would be very cross with Mummy, but at least our dog would not run away any more. Then the phone rang and it was my husband – a meeting was cancelled and he was coming home that night. He arrived at midnight; I had stayed up to make sure our dog was not lying on his back, exposing the evidence.

The next day my then eight-year-old son asked whether the dog had had 'that operation' as he seemed to be quieter, so he had to be let in on the secret too. The next two weeks were spent on continual alert, making sure the dog's tummy was not on display. All went well, and the hair grew back. Now, five years on, we have a fantastic family dog who is beautifully behaved and even has a Gold Citizenship award from the prestigious Kennel Club. He is never far from our sides and goes everywhere on holiday with us. He is the hub of our family. My husband *still* hasn't noticed, and if he hears people talk about that particular operation, he turns to our dog and says proudly: 'You are a lucky boy – thanks to me.'

Although I know I made the right decision, I still feel bad about the deception. And I hope this doesn't rule out the chance of forgiveness, but I should add that the story does not end there. You see, two years later we got a male kitten to add to our family. I think you know where this is going . . . Suffice to say, when I turned up at the vet's, he said, 'Husband away again then?'

Becky

Blame The Buzzards

Dear Simon and the forgiving souls,

My confession goes back to the mid-1990s when my wife and I were happy, carefree, but impoverished newlyweds.

We had moved into our first house, a small cottage by a stream in rural Scotland. Although idyllic, it wasn't exactly spacious, and we dreamed of living somewhere bigger than a shoebox at some stage in the future. But my wife and I, and our two cats, were generally very happy – especially the cats, who had miles of countryside in which to hunt and terrorize the local wildlife.

Our nearest neighbours lived just across the stream in what had been a small, single-storey cottage like ours but had been extended over the years into what was now a large and rather nice house. Our understandable envy was only added to by our neighbour constantly commenting on how small our house was and how he was planning another extension, an extra holiday, another new car. All in all, he was quite an irritating and unpleasant fellow.

As noted, our cats were voracious hunters and brought home little presents for us on a daily basis: mice, birds, you know the type of thing. One advantage of having a stream in front of your house is that gifts of this type are easily disposed of. Simply scoop them up with a shovel and toss them into the water – job done!

Anyway, one day my aim wasn't so great and the unfortunate rodent missed the stream and landed on the roof of our neighbour's conservatory, much to my amusement. Over the coming weeks this 'mistake' became part of my daily routine. Scoop up assorted dead and mauled rodents and deposit skilfully on neighbour's roof. Even the occasional whiff of small rotting corpses and our neighbour's complaints about a local buzzard that kept dropping its prey on his roof didn't make me see sense.

One glorious summer morning I was up and about early, only to find that one of our cats had stumbled across an especially large rabbit some time the night before. This was dead and only partly eaten, and so was dispatched in the same way as all the other presents left by our cats. I went back inside to make breakfast.

I should at this stage mention that I am not seeking forgiveness for the hundreds of small animals our cats killed and maimed over the years. After all, cats do what cats do.

I am not seeking forgiveness for what I did to our neighbour either. I know throwing dead animals on to his roof is not a particularly neighbourly act, but he was a terrible snob and a show-off so I think we are even on this score.

No, I am really seeking forgiveness from our neighbour's nine-year-old daughter. You see, on returning indoors to make breakfast that morning, I heard a scream, then another and another. I rushed back outside to see what was going on, and I could hear the screams coming from our neighbour's open attic window . . .

I am sure you can piece together the sequence of events that led to a nine-year-old girl waking up to find a large, dead, half-eaten rabbit staring at her from her pillow – and to her father cursing and swearing about how awful the local buzzards were.

In mitigation, I should like to point out that the screaming did stop after about an hour and any time I met the daughter afterwards she seemed OK, if a bit nervous of wildlife.

Our neighbour eventually moved house (can't think why), we moved on too, and our cats are long gone. I still have occasional pangs of guilt about my actions, and I hope that by sharing this I can finally rest easy. Am I forgiven?

Steve

Pet Rescue

Hello Father Simon and the Confessions Collective,

Please hear my confession and relieve me of a burden I've carried for many years. This happened as I was walking through a certain city centre from the railway station to my place of work. It's relevant to note that it was a very cold November morning and quite early, so there were few people about. As I made my way along a quiet back street, something on the pavement caught my eye. I stopped and stooped to see what it was. Looking back up at me was a small furry creature. It had puffed up its fur in an apparent attempt to shut out the cold, and it twitched its little whiskers in a pathetic but not unattractive way. It looked very sweet indeed.

By this time, a lady had approached from the opposite direction, stopped and followed my downward gaze. This lady appeared quite well-to-do. She was dressed in a beautiful wool coat, patent-leather court shoes and had tied her scarf in a complicated way like the French do. In short, she was quite posh. Looking intrigued at this bundle of cuddly sweetness, she asked me what it was. Now, Simon, I have no knowledge or expertise in natural history. To this day, I have no idea why I said confidently, 'Oh, it's a chinchilla. Must be a child's escaped pet.'

It was not a residential area, so we were both puzzled how this family pet could have found its way there. 'It'll freeze to death out here, poor thing,' she said. 'What should we do? We can't leave it here. We need to take it to a vet or the RSPCA or something.' Now, not being a particular animal lover, at this point I would have just left it be and gone into work. But I was taken by her compassion and her need to do something. By this time she had picked up the sweet 'chinchilla' and was nursing it in her arms like a baby. It seemed to be perking up from the warmth of her coat and had started playfully to run up and down her arm. Oh, how she seemed to love the little creature, petting it, stroking it, talking to it, even kissing it on its furry little head. She was enraptured. I just stood there, looking on.

Parked near by was a council maintenance truck and in the back was an empty bucket that could have had paint or plaster in it. A plan was forming in my mind – this could be a way of transporting the creature to safety. I tapped on the window to attract the workman's attention. Now, it appears the workman had been observing our actions throughout. He jumped straight out of his seat in what I thought was a commendable eagerness to assist. Perhaps he too could appreciate the lovely little animal.

The kind-hearted woman was now fully occupied keeping control of the revived 'chinchilla', which was attempting to climb inside her coat. They were really bonding. She had a look of joy on her face.

The workman fixed his eyes on the creature and said gruffly, 'I can't believe you've picked that up.'

'Ah, why ever not?' said the woman, tickling the little fellow on the chin playfully (the chinchilla, not the council worker).

'Because it's a sewer rat,' he said.

Now, I don't know which left the woman the fastest, either the rodent formerly known as the 'chinchilla' as she dropped it to the ground, or the blood as it drained from her face. At this point I decided to make my move and mumbled something about being late for work. She looked at me in disappointment and said sadly, tears welling up in her eyes, 'But you told me it was a chinchilla.' Words that still haunt me.

I still think about that lovely lady, and hope she didn't contract some disease from cuddling a creature that had earlier been swimming in, and no doubt eating, the sort of thing to be found in the place after which it got its name. Furthermore, I looked back and saw that even after she'd learned the true identity of our little friend, she was defending the sewer rat from the workman, who was running after it with his shovel. God bless her.

Looking forward to your saintly wisdom.

Bill

Three Little Fishies

Dear All-forgiving Collective,

I am seeking forgiveness not only for myself but also for my brother, the instigator, dare I say mastermind, of this little incident.

It was the summer of 2004. My brother, I shall call him Frank, was back from the army for a few weeks' R&R. He had been in the army for eight years by this point, and being the sort he is, he does everything at 100 per cent and 60 miles an hour, which is probably why he likes the army and they like him. However, when Frank comes home, he likes to chill. And this is where it all began. Frank's favourite kind of relaxation is dangling a hook in the local fishing pond and quietly watching the world go by. In the summer, he would be there from sunrise till sunset. He wouldn't care if he didn't get a bite all day – that, of course, not being the point of the exercise.

This particular summer, there were a few new fishermen in the area, and they liked to compare catches, equipment, cars and so on – basically the opposite of what Frank wanted. All he wanted to do was drown a few maggots and worms and watch the world pass him by before he departed again for foreign climes.

Enter Adrian and his crew; they were the worst. They loved wandering round the pond comparing equipment and offering the sort of advice you already knew or didn't need. Frank, as you can imagine, didn't take kindly to this intrusion on his free time. After several of the regulars had decamped for quieter spots, he decided to enlist my help in remedying the situation.

Frank's plan was simplicity itself, and I have to say the effect was astounding. He positioned me on the main pontoon in the pond, early in the morning before Adrian and his cronies arrived in their 4x4s for another day's heckling and fishing. Before he went, he issued me with the cheapest rod in his collection, a float that to me looked like the kind you get in a cistern, and instructions on what to do. Frank then donned his diving gear and disappeared from sight.

The first thing Adrian and his crew noticed on arrival was a girl of eighteen sitting on the best pontoon with the worst equipment since a bent paperclip and a bit of string tied to your toe. This caused quite a few looks and cackles from them as they set up and started fishing. Within half an hour all four of them had wandered round, tutted at my equipment (one had even suggested to me it was really a man's sport) and asked if I knew what I was doing; they shared some advice with me as well. I was starting to see what Frank disliked about these know-it-alls.

This was the cue Frank had been waiting for. He swam out under the pontoon and put a fish on my hook. He told me later it was quite a large bream. This is when I nearly left, trying to handle a large wriggling fish, until I saw the stunned look on Adrian's face. For the next four hours, every ten to fifteen minutes Frank would swim out and attach another fish to my line. We actually only had three – a bream, a tench and a carp that Frank had acquired the previous day – but as I slipped them into the keep net, Frank would slip them out.

After catching nearly thirty fish that day with my stick and toilet float, I packed up my kit, released my fish from the net and joyfully wandered past Adrian and his stunned mates, who had managed three fish between them all morning, probably as a result of Frank swimming around under the water scaring the pond life away. Frank joined me later having slipped out through a culvert, a little muddy and cold but with the biggest smile on his face I have ever seen.

We do not ask for forgiveness from Adrian and his cronies, or from the pond owner, who inexplicably had a deluge of new paying punters for this prime spot, or from the poor fish. We do, however, ask for forgiveness or at least understanding from the two teenage boys who watched with awe as I landed fish after fish. They too had been teased by Adrian's crew, so perhaps on balance they benefited just as much as Frank.

Thank you, Collective, for listening and for your compassion.

Anne

Rock 'n' Roll

Dear Father Simon and the scientifically minded Collective,

This confession involves the oldest and most accurately dated object in the history of Radio 2 Confessions: a fossil, 180,000,025 years old. (Because this little incident happened twenty-five years ago, and the fossil was a hundred and eighty million years old at the time. Old geologists' joke. The joke, not the geologists. Oh, maybe them as well.)

Back then, in the 1980s, I was a happy and carefree geology undergraduate at the University of Somewhere in the West of England. I was studying a particular rock for my final-year thesis. (An algal mudstone – I know you were wondering.) Part of my research involved going along to the local museum and going 'backstairs' to study specimens from their collection not normally available to the public. That might sound rather dull – I can assure you that indeed it was.

However, this particular sunny afternoon, I found another researcher working in the small, dark and, yes, dusty research room. I knew this lady by sight; she was the very attractive young wife of one of our lecturers. The dark study room suddenly seemed that much brighter. Anyway . . . the day's work involved studying lots of the local fossils known as ammonites. (You know, the curly ones, shaped like a cinnamon whirl.) Some of them were magnificent specimens, as big as soup plates or 12-inch LPs or steering wheels or car tyres . . . you get the picture. And they were jolly heavy. So I fetched the relevant fossils one by one from the shelves of the stockroom, all the while chatting away to Sara (that was not her name). As the hours passed, we got on well, like two young people with a shared fascination in all things geological. The afternoon flew by and all too soon it was time to pack things away.

So I lifted the heavy round fossils one by one and carried

them into the storeroom, then placed them up on the tall shelves. Now, dear listeners, there are a few clues as to what happened next. The words 'heavy', 'round' and 'tall shelves' are clues. Other clues are the absence of words such as 'careful' and 'gravity'. What actually happened next was that I propped up a particularly fine ammonite specimen at one end of the tall shelves. No sooner had I done that than the fossil beastie started to roll along the shelf in a bid for freedom.

There was then an almighty *CRASH!* rather like the sound that several pounds of local limestone makes when hurled at a solid oak table, followed by lots of tinkling as small fragments of ammonite scattered themselves across the table top.

'Are you all right?' came the tender, anxious enquiry from next door.

'Oh, er, fine thanks,' I said.

I carefully, but above all, quickly, tidied up the 180 million pieces of 180-million-year-old fossil and stored them carefully behind another, more solid specimen. I then returned to my fetching and tidying as if nothing had happened. I really didn't want our new platonic relationship to founder just because of some old fossil (and I'm not referring to her husband). But, in fact, I never dared return to the museum and so of course I have never seen the young lady since.

Dear listeners, I beg forgiveness on the basis that it was only a bit of a crush (the young lady) and another bit of crush (the old fossil). And I met and married another even nicer young lady. So there's a happy ending for everyone. Except the fossil.

Sincerely, Malcolm (BSc Geology)

Cat's A Relief

Simon,

I am now in my forties, but in my early twenties I had a pen pal in Germany called Steffi. Steffi became a good friend. She stayed with me and my family in the UK, and vice versa. We were both big fans of a certain stadium rock band, too, and would travel together to watch them play. Some years ago, I visited Steffi in her hometown, as our favourite band were touring Germany. One night we went out for dinner with her boyfriend, and afterwards she dropped me back at her flat and left to spend the night at her boyfriend's place. The bedroom was off the living room, so at 11.30 I got ready for bed, went into the bedroom and shut the door.

I was alone in the flat, apart from Johnny Rotten, Steffi's pet cat, so-called because his fur was ginger, black and white and stuck up on his head like a Mohican – he looked like a little feline punk. At midnight, Johnny started making crazy noises and scratching at my door from the outside. I had a cat myself so I was used to their meows, but Johnny was sounding a little scary and I must admit, Simon, I was frightened. I tried to sleep but he kept on meowing menacingly and scratching. By this point I needed to go to the loo but there was no way I was going to venture out there. I waited for him to go away but he just wouldn't stop. Unable to sleep, by 5 a.m. I was in agony, so I plucked up the courage, got out of bed, opened the door and saw Johnny at my feet. As I made my way across the sitting room, he was walking in front of me calmly. At last, I thought, I could make it to the bathroom.

Out of nowhere another cat, a huge thing at that, leapt off a shelf right in front of my face. I screamed and ran back into the safety of the bedroom. By now I was petrified; the flat was a horror show, full of possessed cats. Still in desperate need of the loo, out of the corner of my eye I spotted a plant in a large pottery container. The container sat on top of a cream-coloured rug. I'm sorry, I had no choice but to let nature take its course, hoping that my friend would never find out and that the plant could take it.

The next day Steffi got back at lunchtime and asked me if I'd slept well. Doing my best to act normally, I said, 'Oh yes, like a baby,' adding casually that I'd been surprised to find out she had a second cat. 'Oh yeah, that's Moggy, he spends most of his time under the bath near the pipes and hardly ever comes out,' she replied, equally casually, as if he was just a normal, unmenacing pet, not the hellish monster who had blighted my sleepless night. Then Steffi walked into her room, whereupon I heard her shout a series of expletives aimed at Johnny Rotten, accusing him in no uncertain terms of failing to use his litter tray. Little did I know that there had been a significant leakage all over her cream wool rug! Little did I also know that this item had been specially imported at great cost to herself, and was a hand-woven one-off. Steffi and I are still in contact, but even to this day she still blames Johnny the cat for destroying her expensive rug, and Moggy has become the cat she shows most affection to.

So I now seek forgiveness – from Steffi for damaging her property, and from Johnny for letting him take the rap for all these years. Am I forgiven?

Tina

A Very Dangerous Liaison

Dear Father Simon and the Collective,

It has been over forty years since my crime, and still it haunts me.

It started with our very large pet dog. We all loved her but my brother was the boss and in charge of caring, feeding, walking and training her. As a younger sister, I was considered too silly to know what to do.

However, not to be outdone, I secretly bought a silent dog whistle and taught the dog to come when she heard the sound. It was great fun. My brother would be making her sit, stay, lie down and every other conceivable trick, and just as he thought he'd cracked it, I would whistle from a secret location. She would, of course, respond, leaving one very annoyed brother, calling her angrily back.

Ho, ho, not so big now, brother, I thought!

It was about this time that my brother found a girlfriend, and dog training sort of got side-lined, as did I, and looking back on it I have to admit I was rather jealous.

We lived with rather strict parents, for whom holding hands was only just about allowed, and so my brother, for reasons I now fully understand but didn't quite then, started to take a very keen interest in long dog walks, mostly in the countryside and always accompanied by his girlfriend. They would be gone for hours and hours but the dog never seemed to look that tired when they returned, which I found slightly odd, as my brother and the girl-friend always looked rather unkempt and a bit flushed.

Somewhat confused by this, I decided to investigate. I secretly followed them on one of their countryside 'dog walks'. At first all seemed well as they went happily towards the farmland on which we traditionally walked the dog, but then they started to change direction, walking not on the path as I had expected, but into some nearby woodland. I continued to follow at a safe distance, hiding behind trees and bushes so as not to be seen.

After a while they stopped and I watched my brother carefully wrap the dog lead round his belt, after which they both disappeared from view. I couldn't see them without revealing myself, and so instead I crouched behind a bush and listened intently, expecting to hear the dog being put through her paces: sit, down, roll over and all the usual instructions. All I heard, though, was silence. Well, there was the odd bit of rustling, but certainly nothing I could identify as training or walking. Eventually I became bored, and so I crept back a bush or two and blew the whistle as hard as I could.

My memory of events from this point is a little hazy, partly I think through shock and confusion, and partly the mounting fear that I had made a big mistake and my brother was going to be very angry. What I do remember was that the dog responded very well to the whistle and set off at a cracking pace towards the source of the sound . . . namely *ME*!

Unfortunately, being dragged behind her was a tangled mess of clothes, arms, legs and ultimately my brother's face, followed somewhat unceremoniously by his rather shocked-looking girlfriend, who was struggling to keep up and untangle herself from my brother and the dog as she ran. The noise was tremendous . . .

I did the only thing that seemed sensible under the circumstances. I ran! Very fast, and I didn't stop until I got home.

Some time later my brother appeared, very dirty, with what looked like the remains of a cowpat on his torn shirt. He said he had fallen down a ditch but I knew better. I don't think the trauma helped his romantic situation either, because the girlfriend was never seen again.

I have never, to this day, had the nerve to admit to this publicly, but I do still feel very guilty . . . for the long-forgotten girlfriend as much as anyone else. The time has now come to seek forgiveness for my sin.

Julie

Birdhouse In My Soul

Dear Father Mayo and assorted members of the confession posse,

I would like to confess to an episode that happened while I was at a northern university. It was something my friends and I found hilarious at the time, but ever since I've felt I should pay penance for the distress I caused to one of my fellow students. I'll call her Lynn.

At first Lynn and I got along famously, studying together and also partaking of the many and varied social opportunities available to us. The problems started when in our second year we decided to rent a house with some other students. What a hoot that would be!

I realized my mistake almost immediately – she was a clean freak. Tidying up, cleaning and, worst of all, hoovering very early (11.00 a.m.) on Saturday and/or Sunday mornings. It drove me mad. I moaned and complained about this unacceptable situation to anyone who would listen, but they just laughed. Even my parents were quite unsympathetic. My resentment of this girl grew unbounded.

Now, Lynn had two lovebirds she kept in a fancy cage in the dining room. They were her pride and joy. She spent hours cleaning them out (of course) and cooing over them. At night she'd let them out to fly around despite knowing I had a bird phobia. I would glare at them – and her – in silence.

One night, after a trip to the local pub, we stopped off at the garage to stock up on essentials – crisps and chocolate – and I bought a packet of mini chocolate eggs. As I was eating them, a devious thought entered my mind. I gently opened the lovebirds' cage door and put two little chocolate eggs in the nest. When Lynn looked next morning she was beside herself with joy.

All she went on about for the next few days was the fact that her birds had laid eggs, and how exciting it would be to bring new life into the world once the chicks hatched. Now, with hindsight, it was at that point I should have come clean and told her the truth, but no, I had to carry on the joke for way too long.

The next weekend, again returning from the pub, I discovered that Lynn's birds had left droppings all over my coursework. During the ensuing argument, I opened the cage door and popped the chocolate eggs into my mouth, saying, 'Ha ha ha, what do you think of that then?' Oh my goodness, Simon, she went ballistic. Realizing that maybe I had overstepped the mark, I tried to explain the eggs were only a 'joke', but as you can imagine nothing I could say or do would calm her down. No amount of apology from me could make her understand or forgive me and I felt dreadful.

Lynn found alternative accommodation after that, and I have felt remorse ever since. Please forgive me my foolish student joke.

Selina

Holidays

We all have rules we live our life by. These are built up over many years and are formed by a variety of influences: the country we live in, our school, our parents and our friends. We learn early on the difference between right and wrong; what is acceptable behaviour and what isn't. We learn that there are consequences to bad or inappropriate behaviour and we adjust our behaviour accordingly.

And then we go on holiday . . .

Slippery When Met

Dear Father Simon,

Before I tell you about my confession, I must enlighten you about an incident that preceded it, which may help you find it in your heart to forgive.

It happened about thirty years ago, when I was ten years old and on holiday with my mum and dad. My father is a competitive man, a trait I have inherited. For us, it made perfect sense to turn the walk from the swimming pool up to the hotel room into a race. This was made all the more exciting by the fact that the route was split into two long corridors with, at one point, flower beds in between. He would take one side and I would take the other. It was by the flower beds that we could see one another. As our holiday progressed, we got better and better at pretending to be calmly walking past the flower beds, then sprinting like mad when out of sight of the other, emerging at the far end in a sedate walk as if it had been a breeze to be the triumphant victor.

I should point out that it was usually Dad who emerged the triumphant victor. He would express his pleasure in winning by throwing his wet towel in my face and shouting, 'POOOOOOEEEEEE!' But on one occasion he shot off early from the last flower bed, which fired me into acceleration. This time I gave it everything I had. I must have won! I could hear his footsteps coming around the corner and he was going to get it. I cried 'POOOOOOEEEEEE!' as I let his losing face have my soggy wet towel.

However, it was not my father's face – he was still by

the flower bed in fits of laughter – but a poor unsuspecting lady's who got the towel. I was devastated – and so was she – but my dad loved it, pleased with his evil deception. But even at the age of ten, I had the idea not to get angry, but to get even.

Luckily my opportunity arose on another holiday, a year or two later. We visited a water park with all the slides and chutes you could wish for. Rather naughtily, my fun-loving dad and I hatched a plan to wait for each other, unseen, inside one of the waterslide tunnels. We did this so we could ride down the rest of the slide together. This was strictly forbidden, so much so that the slides had traffic lights at the top and a guard manning each opening. We pulled our dual-sliding feat off several times. It meant putting your hands and feet on the tunnel roof to stop yourself – quite a skill as by this time you had reached some speed – and holding on tight.

So, picture the scene: the lights went green and Dad went first, disappearing into the tunnel then grinding himself to a halt to wait for me to join him. I could tell he was in place and I awaited the next green light. As the light went from red to green, I had a flash of inspiration. In the queue behind me was a rather large lady waiting for her turn in the slide. Actually, she was bigger than large, she was huge, with bulges in all the wrong places. Being the gentleman-in-training that I was – and still am – I decided to let her go in front of me. How very chivalrous. She happily slid off, and it must have been more than a little surprising to her when she went crashing into my dad inside the tunnel. It must have been equally surprising for him, bearing in mind he was expecting his small son to slow down and join him for a double descent of the rest of the slide, just as before.

Simon, I can honestly say I don't know which was the loudest noise to emerge from the tunnel: her scream, my dad's expletives, or the screeching of his hands on the slide as he frantically tried to accelerate away from the unexpected and unwelcome waterslide co-voyager.

That wasn't the end of it. As you can imagine, the screams alerted the attention of the guard, and that was the end of any water-based activity for my father and me on that holiday. What's more, the lady was less than pleased with my father's behaviour, believing that he had planned this, erm, contact himself. Dad and I were forced to spend the rest of the holiday confined to the table-tennis room, where mischief could be kept to a minimum.

I know what I did was wrong, Father Simon, and I do beg your forgiveness. Not for what I put my father through, because I think he deserved it, but for the poor unsuspecting lady who had the fright of her life.

I await your verdict.

Johnny

Wrong Man Overboard

Dear Simon and the Collective,

I'm writing to seek forgiveness on behalf of a close friend, who for many years was a cruise ship doctor.

As you may know, many elderly passengers take cruises, and it can happen that someone doesn't make it to the end of their trip. Most modern cruise ships, therefore, have on board some sort of facility to cater for such an event. Moreover, some passengers leave instructions at the outset of their journey detailing steps that should be taken if they were to pass on during their trip. One possible request is for burial at sea, a quite legal procedure, which the captain is qualified to oversee.

On this particular occasion, an elderly gentleman, who had a long association with the sea and all things maritime, had made a request for a burial at sea in the event of his passing; and so it came to be. A death on board requiring a burial at sea being thankfully rare, the crew, and my friend the doctor, were inexperienced in such a committal. Everyone concerned was keen to make sure it went without a hitch, and so it was decided that a small party should be assembled prior to the ceremony, with all the equipment needed to carry out the final request, to have a practice run.

With just the doctor and a couple of deck hands in attendance, the body, carefully stitched into a canvas bag, was sombrely carried, with all due respect, up to the deck and placed on the sliding ramp. When the body was safely in place, the mechanism was checked to ensure that all was ready to launch the deceased on his final journey when the time came.

It was at this point that the ship ran unexpectedly into a rather heavy swell. The party decided at once they had better remove the body from the ramp in order to await calmer seas. They began to unfasten it. To their horror, the ship then lurched quite violently to one side, and a vital safety catch – which, being unfamiliar with the equipment, the assembled few had neglected to lock properly into place – clicked loudly, whereupon the canvas bag slid quickly and gracefully away and over the side of the ship.

With no one else there to see what had happened, and the arrival of the captain and other mourners imminent, a quick decision had to be made . . .

The most junior rating was sent down to the kitchen and returned with two 50kg bags of potatoes. These were quickly sewn into another canvas body bag, which was placed back on the ramp, this time with the safety catch secured correctly, just in time.

The service was carried out and, to the best knowledge of all present, the gentleman was sent on his way with dignity. Neither the captain nor the mourners ever knew they'd paid their last respects to 100 kilograms of King Edwards.

Do you think, all these years later, forgiveness might be forthcoming? After all, the final wish of the elderly gentleman was granted, albeit slightly prematurely.

Jim

'Is It A Bird?'

Dear Simon,

My confession goes back nine years, but is still in my thoughts to this day.

We were a very active family and packed in as many weekend breaks as our budget allowed. We loved camping, but after this incident we no longer did it so often.

It was Whitsuntide half-term and we had gone away for a long weekend to Scotland, to camp on the banks of a loch. The weather was as expected – wet – and all the sorts of things a family with a six-year-old and an eight-year-old on board would need had been carefully packed into our hatchback. The campsite was fully equipped with showers, washing-up stands, washing machines and flushing toilets. The views across the loch were wonderful. There was even an on-site restaurant, which was most welcome.

We had a nice evening meal and both boys were very excited to be sleeping under canvas. The evenings were very light, so we kept them up playing pool, snap and I-spy, anything to keep them going until we could see they were fit to drop, then we settled them down for the night.

Around midnight I was woken by my eldest son, shaking me furiously, whispering that he was desperate for the toilet and couldn't hold on any longer. There had been a lot of juice consumed over the extended evening so perhaps this wasn't so surprising. Feeling a little disorientated, I unzipped the tent door very quietly and slipped out. Out of the corner of my eye, and quite close to our tent, I noticed a white swan on the loch-side. As I helped my son from the tent, I heard the swan make a faint squawk. We turned and caught a glimpse of its backside, disappearing down into the loch.

We tiptoed to the toilet block and back without incident,

settled into our sleeping bags and drifted off into dreamland. Some time later, in the early hours, I was awoken by loud voices all around our tent. As I gradually came to, I became aware of large vehicles pulling up, the sound of two-way radios and, in the distance, the unmistakable *whup-whup* of a helicopter.

I crawled towards the tent door to take a look. To my amazement, there was an ambulance, a paramedic and a small crowd gathered just a few metres from our tent. I was about to remind them that this was a campsite and small children were trying to sleep, when I heard the paramedic talking to his colleague. 'You finish immobilizing the leg and the chopper should be in place to lift him.'

I had a flashback to what I had seen– or thought I had seen – earlier that night. Surely not . . . It was a swan, wasn't it? I had to ask what had happened.

'Some chap was walking back to his tent when something startled him and he slipped down the bank on to the rock at the bottom. We think he's been down there hours, but nobody could hear him.'

I had a sinking feeling in the pit of my belly. The following day, the talk on the site was all about this poor man. 'Did he slip or was he pushed?' I even heard at one point. Stories ranged wildly from a broken leg to hypothermia and the need for life-saving medical intervention.

Now, as all parents will appreciate, children should never be entrusted with a secret, and this was not going to be an exception. My son was clearly mulling the whole event over in his mind when, without warning, he blurted out, in the small campsite shop, that the swan we had startled was clearly not a swan at all but was obviously the man who had fallen into the loch. Everyone stopped what they were doing and stared at me in disgust. Needless to say, we packed our things and left as soon as we could.

I would like to take this opportunity to apologize to the individual concerned and I sincerely hope he did not have too long a stay in hospital.

I fall upon the mercy of the Ecclesiastical Collective.

Stacy

The Big Stink

Simon,

My confession dates back to 1993 when, as a young and aspiring business studies teacher in a comprehensive school, I organized an exchange visit for around twenty of my sixth-formers to Gothenburg.

Despite my lack of experience in organizing anything, the week-long visit went extremely well and a good time was had by all. Well, with one exception. A young man by the name of Jeremy, he was far too worldly-wise and sophisticated to 'enjoy' anything and spent all day, every day, making sarcastic comments like, 'How exciting to go on a tram' or, 'Gosh, that was good, I really understood what they were saying' when we got to appear on a Swedish TV show, an opportunity the other members of the party were rightly thrilled about. Even being given VIP tickets to the reopening of the Liseberg amusement park in the centre of Gothenburg failed to draw a favourable response from Jeremy, who declared it 'childish'.

As you can imagine, this started to grate after a few days, and I am ashamed to say I hatched a cruel plan to exact revenge on him. The Swedes 'enjoy' (and I use that word carefully) a delicacy called surströmming, which is basically a tin of rotten, fermented herring. It apparently tastes delicious but the stink it emits is so vile it is, I'm told, an offence to open a tin in a public place. Well, my colleagues and I decided to buy a tin (at considerable personal expense, it must be said).

On the 24-hour boat trip back, we passed the time by undertaking a light-hearted mock 'awards ceremony', where every member of the party got a gong for something, such as 'biggest diplomatic gaff', 'worst dressed' and so on. But we saved the best until last. To conclude the event we announced a special prize draw for a wonderful Swedish delicacy, and I bigged up just how delicious, special and expensive this delicacy was. I got one of the other teachers to draw a name from the hat and, guess what, Jeremy 'won'. He accepted the prize with all his usual lack of grace, the irritating little so-and-so.

Simon, I ask for forgiveness, not for getting my own back on Jeremy, who really did deserve it (and is probably now a perfectly decent, well-adjusted adult human being), but for the distress I must have caused his poor mother. It seems that, upon opening the 'strange tin of Swedish tuna' that Jeremy had given her as a gift from his trip, the ensuing stink was so unimaginably bad that it induced instant sickness and she had to have her entire house fumigated.

Martin

The Road to Smell

Simon,

A long, long time ago – well, 1985 – I was an au pair working in France. In those pre-Channel Tunnel days I used to travel across by coach and ferry. It was quite an arduous journey that took fifteen hours, and I preferred to travel at night in the hope of sleeping most of the way and so being oblivious to the uncomfortable seats and annoying passengers.

Most of the time I was lucky enough to sit next to someone who, like me, just wanted some shut-eye in the hope of getting the whole thing over with as painlessly as possible. On one particular occasion I wasn't so lucky and found myself squashed into a corner by a large, smelly, chatty man. I tried to do the decent thing and politely engaged in conversation, hoping that if I didn't reply very enthusiastically and yawned a lot he would eventually give up.

It was soon clear that he wasn't going to do anything of the sort and, because I was so uncomfortable, even if he did I wouldn't get any sleep anyway. Finally, between Calais and Paris, the coach made a pit-stop. Many of the passengers got off to stretch their legs.

After walking around a deserted service station for ten minutes, I got back on the coach. There was no sign of my neighbour. The driver asked if everyone was back on board, but I couldn't speak. My mind was in turmoil. I don't know whether it was the prospect of some much-needed peace or the possibility of being able to breathe through my nose again, but I said nothing. Maybe he'd only been going this far anyway. However, as we set off and I stretched out my legs into the now empty space next to me, I looked out of the window and saw the man running across the car park, waving frantically as we drove off into the night.

I never attempted to get the driver to stop. I couldn't think of a plausible reason why I hadn't noticed the man was missing in the first place. When I got off the coach in the cold light of a Paris dawn, I legged it to the Metro before the driver realized the owner of the one remaining suitcase was not there to pick it up. To make matters worse, as I made my escape I noticed a large family group gradually becoming forlorn as they waited for someone to appear from the vehicle, who, of course, never did.

I now meekly seek forgiveness for leaving a poor man stranded in a foreign motorway service station in the dead of night. There is nothing I can say in my own defence except that I didn't get any sleep on the remainder of the journey either, and have been haunted by the vision of him running after us ever since.

Maggie

It's All A Bit of A Blur

Simon,

Many years ago I worked in travel publishing and had the great advantage of seeing the world at the company's expense. I was particularly lucky to look after Australia as a territory and often travelled there on business.

At the time the MD's secretary was an attractive woman in her early twenties, who decided to take two years off to travel the world with a friend. On the day she left, she asked me when I was next going to be Down Under. It was in three months' time, and it just happened to coincide with when she was going to be in the same part of the country, so she made me promise to look her up when I got there.

Well, the time came, and we arranged to meet for a catch-up – all very innocent.

After a drink and a great dinner, we went to a bar, and as the evening wore on we were getting pretty merry. By the time we left she'd missed her last bus home so she said she would call her flatmate, I assumed to get a lift. After phoning, she announced she was staying the night at my hotel, some-what to my surprise, but not displeasure. Luckily, the hotel had upgraded me to a junior suite, so there was plenty of room.

Well, Simon, we were both very tired and somewhat squiffy, so we decided to hit our separate sacks. She said she needed something to put her contact lenses in, so I suggested she leave them in a glass of water in the bath-room. Now, this was years ago and people mainly wore hard contact lenses, and because of the expense often only had one pair, and such was the case here.

During the night, I became very thirsty and wandered into the bathroom to find a lovely glass of refreshing water awaiting me. You can probably see the next bit coming – yes, I drank the water, complete with contact lenses. Realizing what I had done, I refilled the glass and returned to the bedroom where she was still sleeping soundly.

Come the morning there was a shriek of 'Where are my lenses?' I rushed in and, mustering my best innocent act, said, 'But I thought you put them in a glass of water,' to which she replied she was certain she had. I pointed to the floor below where the glass was positioned, where there was a conveniently placed drain, presumably there to protect the room should the bath overflow. I told her that she was so drunk the previous night that she must have dropped the lenses, and they were now probably well on the way towards the city's sewer outlet.

She was very upset. Under her insurance scheme, the small print of which I had to kindly read aloud to her, it would take six to eight weeks to get replacements from the UK. She had glasses, but they were broken. Like a true gentleman, I commiserated, and suggested she contact her UK optician as soon as possible. How helpful of me.

Well, Simon, though I really should have confessed at the time, and perhaps contributed financially to the lenses' replacement, I ask for forgiveness based on the fact that drinking them in the first place was an unintentional act. I am very, very sorry that my action caused her to spend nearly eight weeks abroad with reduced vision.

Matt

PS I know some listeners will be wondering this, so I have to say I never saw the lenses again.

Motormouth

Dear Father Simon and the Collective,

I humbly seek forgiveness for something that happened in the Swinging Sixties, although I hardly dare hope for leniency from the Mother Superior.

I was a young man who had recently purchased a very snazzy Ford Zephyr convertible. It was lilac with leather seats, and the back seat was flat and seemed to go on for ever – it was a real babe magnet! In those irresponsible days, nobody bothered with seat belts – this was before it became the law to wear one – and it was quite usual to sit on other people's laps, which meant you could fit lots of people into this car, especially when the roof was down.

One fine day, I was cruising around town with a few mates when we noticed four very lovely lady hitch-hikers. What else were we to do but give the lovely ladies a lift? They happily accepted, and it was cosy in the car, to say the least. There were long limbs everywhere, Simon!

A beautiful blonde next to me leaned across and whispered, 'Oh, I love your car. Where did you get it?'

An idea popped into my head and came out just as fast from my mouth. 'I bought it with the royalties from our last single.'

'Single?' she said, looking extremely interested. 'Are you famous?'

'You might have heard of us,' I said. 'We're the Hollies.'

At this point all the girls swooned and screamed and were more than happy to hang out with us for the rest of the evening. (I should remind people that this was back in the days of grainy black and white TV, and the girls perhaps hadn't got as good a look at the real Hollies as they might otherwise have done.)

However, the wheels very nearly came off when they asked us to sing 'Bus Stop' to them, high in the Hit Parade at the time, which we did very badly, blaming laryngitis and sore throats from too much rehearsal singing. Luckily, they believed us.

So, Simon, I beg forgiveness from the four young ladies who thought they had been out with the famous Hollies and probably regale their own families with the tale to this day – and from the real Hollies for abusing their name and fame . . .

Billy

A *Lie of Descent*

Dear Father Simon and the Assembled Collective,

Whilst listening to the confession of the 'Hollies' imperson-
ators recently, I felt compelled to offer my own, related sin.

My name is Roger Anthony. Or, as our American
cousins call me, 'An-tho-knee'. My confession dates back to
1980 when my wife and I were on a road trip in the US. It
began in a small town (in Georgia, I think) where, as I signed
a credit-card slip, the assistant looked at my name and
asked, 'Are you related to Suzy B?'

Never having heard of the lady, I said no. But everywhere I went, I kept getting asked the same question. It
seemed some research was necessary. Via a local library (no
internet in those days!), I discovered Susan B. Anthony was
a key figure of the American women's suffrage movement
and hugely celebrated. Indeed, a Susan B. Anthony dollar
coin had recently been issued.

Thus, when next asked the question, I said indeed I was
– and claimed to be her great-great-great-grandson on a
visit to the US! The woman behind the counter shrieked and
insisted on giving us our groceries for nothing.

Thinking this a bit weird we offered our thanks and left.
The following day in another small town I was asked again,
was I related to Suzy B? Convinced they would twig, I – to
my shame, yet tantalized by the prospect of further 'freebies'
– replied, 'Yes, I am her great-great-great-great-grandson' (I
kept losing count of how many 'greats' I would need in order
to be related to someone born in the 1820s). This time we not

only got free food but the offer of free accommodation as well. My wife and I were beginning to enjoy this. Still, we couldn't believe no one had cottoned on – especially as the lady in question had never married or had children.

However, matters came to a head a couple of days later. Driving further south, we arrived at a town where we discovered a carnival was on. There was bunting along the street, the mayor was on a podium and there was a huge barbecue – complete with the high school band and cheer-leaders strutting their stuff. Everyone was having a great time, and after parking our hire car we joined the throng on the pavement.

We asked what the carnival was in aid of, and were told that somebody from the town we'd just come from had phoned his cousin (his cousin being the mayor of the town we'd just arrived in) to say Susan B. Anthony's (insert as many greats as you like here) grandson was on his way. The mayor had therefore decided to organize an impromptu welcoming party to greet us.

At this point, my wife and I – but mainly my wife – decided enough was enough. We slunk away, stopping at a phone booth to call the local police station and inform them that due to a tight schedule, Susan B's great-great-great-great-great-grandson would not be able to visit but hoped the townsfolk enjoyed their day.

I thus ask for forgiveness for taking advantage of what, in retrospect, was the generosity and kind spirit of many Americans – some of whom may have recounted to their children, or even grandchildren, or dare I say great-grand-children, their meeting with a distant relative of Susan B. Anthony.

Roger Anthony

The Brazen Beach Burials

Dear Father Simon and the Collective,

As a student in the early 1990s, I filled my summers working as a sailing instructor in France for a well-known company offering week-long activity holidays to school groups. As students, we were offered transport, a tent to sleep in and food. A pittance of a wage was thrown in for good measure. However, it is amazing how far a measly wage will spread when you can fill a bucket with wine at a vineyard for a few quid. Early one summer, after plentiful imbibing, we saw a large campervan, replete with satellite dish and every extra appendage imaginable, parked on the beach at the end of the winding, unmade road leading to our campsite.

This was not unusual, as the main holiday parks in the area closed at 10.00 p.m. on the dot, and any European holidaymakers having made the long pilgrimage often arrived late and parked up anywhere before gaining entry to the site in the morning.

On surfacing for work the following day, we were greeted by plumes of golden sand flying into the air, accompanied by the revving of a big diesel engine, as said pantechnicon of comfort was well and truly beached up to its axles in sand – and going nowhere.

We took pity on the new arrivals. Requisitioning the site tractor, we drove carefully down to the beach and after a brief introduction hooked up to the campervan and pulled out the somewhat embarrassed Germans, sending them happily on their way. Before they left, we were presented with a tip of around £50 – almost a week's wages. As you can imagine, we were elated.

It wasn't long before the elation was replaced by the sin of greed. Seeing a lucrative business opportunity, we started to keep a more watchful eye on the area. It seemed that the 'camper on the beach' problem, far from being a one-off, occurred at least two or three times a week and so the spot quickly became a regular detour on the way home from the pub in the early hours. Early the following morning we would appear, complete with tractor and tow rope, and rescue the grateful tourists, each time being rewarded with a small but very welcome financial token of their esteem.

The weeks went by and the 'added income' became increasingly essential in funding our now comfortable leisure lifestyle.

One evening, though, after a disappointing two stranded vehicles in a month, we sat glumly at the bar considering our options. The kitty was dangerously low. It was then that the master plan was hatched.

Why wait for the vans to sink naturally when, with a little effort and without causing suspicion, we could help them on their way?

We hurried home and sure enough, there was a vehicle at the end of the track, but not quite far enough down that it would require our assistance the next day.

What followed was a group of young men, in the dead of the mild French night, frantically digging sand away from the stable rear wheels of a van with their bare hands, and the subsequent inexorable sinking of the offending vehicle up to its axles. (How the occupants never woke with all the drunken shushing and digging going on, I will never know.)

Roll on 8.00 a.m., and out came the tractor and a brazen request for £50 or £100 for a tow (we eventually decided the amount depending on the glamour and assumed price of the sabotaged vehicle). 'It's company policy' was always our catchphrase (in somewhat broken French), once the vehicle was hitched up and before the tow began.

I lost count of the number of times we repeated this deception, and when added to the income from the genuinely stranded vehicles, the result was several hundred pounds a week for each of us all summer long. The total take during the season must have run into thousands.

So, Father Simon, I'd like now to apologize to all manner of German, Dutch and Belgian tourists who suffered at the hands of our skulduggery. In mitigation, however, I should add that the only real damage was to their wallets and their pride, and their children always enjoyed a brief ride on the tractor too.

Can you find it in your hearts to forgive this entrepreneurial exercise?

Northern Clive